CULTURE RULES!

The 10 Core Principles of Corporate Culture

and how to use them
to create greater business success.

"Culture rules! And Culture has rules!"

*"If you don't understand your corporate culture,
you don't understand your business".*

John R Childress

Culture Rules!
The 10 Core Principles of Corporate Culture
and how to use them to create greater business success

Published by The Principia Group 2017

ISBN: 978-0-9575179-9-8

Printed by Lightning Source

For speaking engagements, consulting, or other business matters, contact:

John R Childress

Email: john@johnrchildress.com

This wonderful book will transform our understanding of corporate culture. Seeing culture as a business system, and the 10 Core Principles that govern culture, can help leaders at all levels develop a high-performance organization. Finally, an approach to corporate culture that makes a compelling business case!

~Stephen M. R. Covey,
*The New York Times bestselling author of **The Speed of Trust**, and co-author of **Smart Trust***

Acknowledgments

I must thank all my clients who over the past 35 years have allowed me to explore with them the intricacies and complexities of their companies, their leadership teams and their business and personal lives.

My understanding of corporate culture is largely the result of their openness and constant encouragement to find solutions that stick, and that will improve the lives of people and the performance of organizations.

While too many to list here, I must single out Frank Tempesta, Richard Millman, Demetrie Comnas, Ron Burns, Ian Walsh, Lewis Booth and David Schoch for their exceptional wisdom over the years about business, people and teams. I must also give thanks to Stephen M R Covey and Jerry Miller for their insightful comments and suggestions on the manuscript.

Also a huge thank you to Christiane Wuillamie, OBE, a highly successful entrepreneur, turnaround specialist, and business leader who has given great advice and counsel in putting this book together.

And then there is my cat, Sibelius, who keeps me company and provides great entertainment during long days and nights of research and writing.

To You, the reader . . .

I think of this book as a mirror that reflects back the good news and the bad news about business and corporate culture. If after a hard look into this mirror, you decide to tackle the challenges of leading and shaping your corporate culture, I hope these few core principles and the chapters on their application to real business challenges will serve as a useful guidebook and roadmap to greater business results, customer satisfaction and employee engagement.

John R Childress
London 2017

Table of contents

Introduction

 Culture eats strategy for breakfast!

This quote pops up in nearly every article written about corporate culture in the last decade. The saying went viral following a 2006 Wall Street Journal article about then Ford executive Mark Fields and his "Way Forward" team, tasked to reshape the old Ford culture.[1] It was reported that a large banner bearing the quote hung in the culture change war room at Ford headquarters.

Like many popular management mantras, the phrase *"culture eats strategy for breakfast"* is both catchy and shallow. This maxim looks great in PowerPoint presentations and slogans, but is not very helpful in furthering the concept of corporate culture as a useful tool to improve business performance, productivity and employee engagement.

Whenever someone asks me about the phrase *"Culture eats strategy for breakfast"*, I usually counter with my version, born from 35 years of working with businesses large and small on the issues of culture, leadership and strategy execution.

Culture and Strategy sit down to breakfast together, build a joined-up plan, engage all levels of the organization, then go to work.

Any seasoned business executive understands that a good strategy delivered by a poor culture is a business failure waiting to happen, just as a poor strategy can end in business disaster no matter how good the culture. The fact is, strategy and culture are interdependent. Two sides of the same coin. Both are important in the quest for superior performance and one without the other is akin to a Ferrari with four flat tires.

Yet of the two, corporate culture is the least understood. For being such a popular business term (especially with consultants and the business press), corporate culture is still a mystery to most C-suite executives, managers and Boards, and even among business academics it remains poorly understood. There is no standard or agreed-upon definition and on the market today there are currently over 70 different corporate culture assessments, each purporting to diagnose your real culture. And even the large global consulting and executive search firms are now offering culture surveys and culture change programs.

At a recent World Knowledge Forum is Seoul, South Korea, most of the presentations focused on Asian macro-economic and geopolitical issues. Yet in nearly every discussion the issues of corporate culture, national culture, culture change, culture for innovation, integrating different cultures and developing an international corporate culture rang out from the speakers and from audience questions. A 2016 Deloitte global study of business leaders and executives revealed that only 12% believe their companies are driving the "right culture" and a whopping 72% say they don't fully understand their own company culture.[2] The same study also estimates that close to 50% of companies are either engaged in or thinking about reinforcing or reshaping their corporate culture for competitive advantage.

Why the global interest in corporate culture? Simple really. Culture impacts business performance, both positively and negatively. And it has a major impact on the effectiveness of cross-border M&A and the ability of national companies to operate globally. More and more, business is becoming a global game. The ability to understand the strengths and weaknesses of your own corporate culture, understand the impact of national culture and to learn the skills of reshaping culture to fit changing business strategies and global expansion is critical to sustained success.

It pays to understand what culture is, where it comes from and the levers for culture change.

After over 35+-years consulting and advising on corporate culture and performance, I have run into many examples of costly business mistakes resulting from a lack of understanding of corporate culture. Here are a few examples out of many.

The Culture of Banking is Broken

 The financial crisis is a stark reminder that transparency and disclosure are essential in today's marketplace. ~Jack Reed

The *"casino culture"* of banking was a major cause of the 2009 global economic crisis when their excessive risk behavior, outright fraud, rate manipulation, miss-selling and maniacal focus on the development and sales of high-profit investment products began to unravel, resulting in several major bankruptcies and multiple fines for fraudulent and criminal activities. A total of over $300 billion in fines have been levied against major banks between 2009 and 2016. And the resulting increase in banking regulations, external audits and a greater number of compliance requirements have not substantially changed the culture inside banks nor stopped their reckless behavior.

In 2016 Wells Fargo, considered the darling of the banking industry for many years due to its high profitability, was charged with setting up over 1.5 million fake banking accounts and 565,000 credit cards not authorized by their customers so that bank staff could meet management-imposed sales quotas. A culture of *"make your quota or leave"*, along with a leadership culture of arrogance and pressure tactics on staff led to the resignation of the CEO and $185 million in fines, including a $100 million penalty from the Consumer Financial Protection Bureau, the largest such penalty the agency has issued.[3] And this fraudulent practice had been going on for over 5 years, even with the added scrutiny of the regulators. A good example of the fact that you cannot regulate behavior and corporate culture from the outside in.

You might ask why disgruntled and pressured bank staff rarely speak up about fraudulent practices, money-laundering, illegal trading and excessive profits in their organization? What you will learn in this book is that culture works on human logic, not business logic, and peer pressure is one of the strongest drivers of corporate culture.

In a study from Deloitte Australia, financial services firms that focus on improving culture instead of adding additional compliance systems perform better on compliance audits.[4] The study believes $240 billion is wasted on overly-complex compliance systems, when a *"culture of compliance"* is actually more effective.

Fly the Friendly Skies?

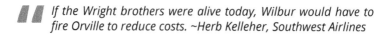 *If the Wright brothers were alive today, Wilbur would have to fire Orville to reduce costs. ~Herb Kelleher, Southwest Airlines*

Another example where business mistakes have been made due to a poor understanding of the power of corporate culture comes from a different industry. Two large international airlines, United and Delta, both decided to compete with the growing popularity of budget airlines by starting their own branded budget airline. The strategy was to capture the budget minded traveler with the power of their well-established brand in a no-frills airline. Millions were spent on advertising, new planes with new paint jobs, new logos and additional crew. Cost savings would come from using the airport infrastructure of their already established parent company, smaller planes and less frills. Delta's Song brand started operations in 2003 and United's TED brand in 2004. Both budget brands launched to great fanfare. However, both ceased operations only a few years later, unable to turn a profit.

While executives at both United and Delta blamed the demise on rising fuel prices, already established budget airlines, like Southwest and Jet Blue, continued to operate profitably. The back story of this example is that the imbedded rule-based culture, large-company bureaucracy and business processes designed for a global carrier were counter-cultural to the team-based, no-frills but extra-friendly *"human service"* ethos of a successful budget airline.

And just to punctuate the point of corporate culture and its impact, United Airlines recently forcefully dragged and ejected a passenger from a plane before take-off from Chicago due to overbooking, creating a media backlash that reduced its market value by over $1.8 billion. According to an immediate public response from the CEO of United, the crew were just following the rules established for overbooking. However, in a subsequent open letter to United customers and the general public, CEO Oscar Munoz stated: *"It happened because our corporate policies were placed ahead of our shared values. Our procedures got in the way of our employees doing what they know is right*.[5]

And Delta, another global airline with a rule-based culture, charged a unit of soldiers returning from Afghanistan over $2,800 for excess baggage, which drew an outcry from social media after two Staff Sergeants posted a complaint on YouTube. Delta has a three free bag rule for military personnel traveling in coach class. One of the Staff Sergeants explained in the video that his fourth bag was his weapons case, containing his M4 rifle, a 203 grenade launcher and a 9-millimeter handgun. Not suitable carry-on luggage! *"A $200 bill for extra baggage by a government-contracted airline is the worst welcome home any soldier could receive"*, Joe Davis, a spokesman for Veterans of Foreign Wars, said in a statement. In response, Delta said on its blog that it was *"continuing to work with the soldiers individually to make this situation right for each of them"*.[6]

Contrast this with the recent incident where Southwest Airlines, known for its culture of LUV and customer care, turned a plane around on the tarmac, went back to the gate and escorted a female passenger off and booked her onto another Southwest flight when the pilot learned that her son had been seriously hurt in an accident and was in a coma. They even delivered her luggage to her new hotel. Again, a difference in cultures. Service and compassion vs schedule and rules.

The Corporate Culture System and Core Principles

 Finance requires understanding financial matters, but management is different - it requires understanding complex systems, how they operate, the nature of organizations, what happens when people interact in groups and how to motivate and guide people. ~Rosabeth Moss Kanter

In my 35 years of working with businesses large and small on the issues of culture, leadership and strategy execution, I have learnt that culture is not an isolated element or an HR issue. Corporate culture is an end-to-end business system. And like any functioning business system, it is built, sustained and reshaped according to a set of rules. Culture Rules. Those who understand the rules and operating principles that govern the corporate culture system gain access to a set of powerful levers for improving business performance, customer satisfaction and employee engagement. Those who ignore the rules of culture often find the path to exceptional performance both elusive and costly.

In my previous book, *LEVERAGE: The CEO's Guide to Corporate Culture*, I took a practitioner's scalpel to the entire corporate culture movement; from culture assessments to culture change methodologies to culture consultants.[7] My goal was to help CEOs and business leaders better understand their own corporate culture and how it influences, both positively and negatively, tangible business performance. A review in *The Economist* magazine called my book one of the most *"sensible efforts in an otherwise charlatan-infested field"*.[8]

In the years since the publication of *LEVERAGE* I have received many emails and letters from readers urging me to provide even more clarity and useable business applications relating to corporate culture and business performance. This book is my attempt to provide more insights and business applications pertaining to the impact of corporate culture on business performance and employee engagement.

I have organized this book into three sections. Section One presents the 10 Core Principles of Corporate Culture with explanations and examples. Section Two focuses on how to Leverage these core principles when leaders are confronted with business challenges. Again I have used both current and historic examples to show how the principles of corporate culture can improve the odds of business success. Lastly is an Epilogue, which poses a series of thought provoking corporate culture questions that every business leader should think about and discuss with their team.

My goal throughout is to provide the reader with specific and useful insights on how they can use these principles to build a stronger, more sustainable, more profitable organization with engaged and enthusiastic staff. A better understanding of these core principles could prove to be a significant platform for sustainable success and competitive advantage.

 Running an organization without an understanding of corporate culture is like driving a speeding car using only the rear view mirror.

My Corporate Culture Journey

> **❚❚** *The journey of a thousand miles*
> *begins with just a single step. ~Confucius*

The other day I was talking with one of my clients in Australia who is building a culture of high performance and accountability, delivering stellar financial results and high levels of employee engagement. During the conversation he asked *"What caused you to spend your life studying, speaking and consulting on the importance of corporate culture?"*

Believe it or not, in over 35 years as a management consultant and business author, that was the first time I had been asked that simple, yet profound question. The easy answer is that I find it interesting and challenging. The real answer goes back to a pivotal experience as a college junior-year-abroad student at the American University of Beirut, Lebanon in 1968-69. I didn't know it then, but that year put me on a path to study and learn all I could about group behavior, leadership, culture and change.

Beirut was paradise when I first arrived in August, 1968 as a Junior-Year-Abroad student from the University of California, Riverside to study at the American University of Beirut. The world had nicknamed Beirut the *"Paris of the Middle East"*, for its wide boulevards lined with haute couture shops and outdoor cafes with menus in French and Arabic. Wealthy families

---

from all over the Middle East sent their sons and daughters to AUB for a Western-style education. My roommate in the dormitory on campus not only spoke English, Arabic, French and Armenian, he was a Palestinian of Armenian ancestry and very wise in the ways of international politics, something a young man like me from a small town in California had no clue about.

During the first semester my newfound college friends and I swam in the Mediterranean Sea and skied on the slopes of the majestic mountains overlooking the metropolis of Beirut, sometimes all in the same day! I met a large number of international students and became friendly with many. We all seemed to share the same views and values about life, education, the future, and of course, girls. In 1968, Beirut was like any other modern Mediterranean seaside city: full of life, seaside cafes, girls in mini-skirts and admiring young men.

On December 28th, 1968, Israeli commandos landed in helicopters just outside the Beirut International Airport fences in the middle of the night, blew up 13 Middle East Airlines planes parked on the tarmac and shot out windows in the terminal. The raid was in reprisal for Lebanon sheltering Palestinian refugees, whom the Israelis considered terrorists. They left 45 minutes later with no loss of life on either side. At that moment, Beirut, AUB and my life changed forever.

The very next day I flew into Beirut International Airport on a Turkish Airlines flight from my Christmas holidays with friends in Istanbul. The still-smoldering remains of burned out jetliners were in clear view and the Lebanese army was out in full force, with multiple checkpoints on the roads back to the University.

Needless to say, our cozy college world was turned upside down. For the rest of the year there were armed guards, student demonstrations, and terrorist activity across the city. I saw first-hand how hatred and irrational beliefs on both sides could ruin a once-prosperous and powerful trading city.

What hit me the hardest was how many of my Arab student friends at the University subsequently changed. I'm not certain they changed their core values, but they certainly changed their behavior. Many of them traded in their books and guitars for Uzis and AK-47s and left school. Most I never heard from again.

This radical change in behavior haunted me. What caused their behavior to change so dramatically? There seemed to be a social phenomenon going on that I didn't understand. I stayed at AUB amid all the riots, finished out the school year and went back to California to pursue my original studies in marine biology, but I wasn't the same person. After a Masters at Harvard and then Ph.D. studies at the University of Hawaii, I still couldn't shake the experience. I needed to figure this out.

Building a Consulting Firm

 Experience isn't the best teacher; it is the only teacher!
~Dr. Albert Schweitzer

While in my last year of PhD studies in marine biology in Hawaii, at the urging of a friend I attended a seminar on human behavior and group dynamics. During this seminar, a series of light bulbs went off for me, as I learnt that people behave differently in groups than when alone and social networks and peer pressure are some of the most powerful modifiers of human behavior. I dug into all the research I could find, learned about organizational dynamics and co-founded The Senn-Delaney Leadership Consulting Group in 1978, all to further explore and consult on the nascent field of team behavior in business, organizational dynamics and business process improvement.

My first practical indoctrination into the impact and importance of corporate culture on business performance came a year and a half later, when I received a call from Phil Clark, the new President of General Public Utilities Company, owner and operator of the Three Mile Island Nuclear Power Station in Harrisburg, Pennsylvania. In the early morning hours of March 28, 1979, TMI Unit 2 suffered an accident where radioactive steam was released into the atmosphere along with a partial melt down of the core reactor. It was the first accident at a US nuclear plant and quickly made national and international headlines. The TMI melt-down became the largest media event since the assassination of JFK 15 years earlier and effectively dealt a death blow to the hopes of nuclear energy replacing fossil fuels in the US.

Phil Clark and many members of the new management team he recruited following the accident were from the US Nuclear Navy. When you are down in a nuclear submarine for weeks on end, safety and human behavior are your most pressing concerns. The Nuclear Navy knew a lot about group behavior and a safety culture and Phil wanted help in creating the same culture at TMI. Over the next three years my team and I interviewed managers and workers, developed culture change workshops and helped refine a new vision based on safety and accountability. I am proud to say that TMI-2 has been successfully decommissioned and TMI-Unit 1 is back in full operation with one of the most productive and safest operating records of any nuclear plant in the world.

What we discovered during our initial analysis at TMI was a corporate culture of strong, independent departments and business functions which didn't trust or communicate well with each other. We began to refer to them as *silos*, standing next to, but independent of each other. We also discovered a culture of managerial arrogance based on the belief that there was no need for continuous safety training with all the redundant back-up systems built into the physical design of the plant. The President's Commission Report on the TMI Nuclear Accident concluded that the accident was ultimately the result of a weak safety culture and human error.

Our consulting firm continued to grow and learn more and more about corporate culture. Then in 1984 Tom Peters and Bob Waterman, two former McKinsey consultants, published the NY Times bestseller *In Search of Excellence* in which they argued that corporate culture is strongly linked to exceptional business performance.

Suddenly corporate culture was a hot topic and my consulting firm was in great demand. We opened offices in Los Angeles, New York and London and worked on some of the biggest culture change projects, including the shift in McDonalds from a process-centric to a customer-centric culture, developing a competitive culture in the new "Baby Bells" after the breakup of the US Bell Telephone monopoly, the explosive growth of Yum! Brands, the transformation of British Gas TransCo and the successful turnarounds of Navistar and the Ford Halewood automotive plant.

In 2001 I retired from Senn-Delaney and took time to rethink all I had learned. What did I learn from this quiet reflection time in the South of France? There was still a great deal about corporate culture, group behavior, leadership and business performance improvement that I didn't fully understand!

Two years later I begin independent consulting and advisory work, which culminated in two books, *LEVERAGE: The CEO's Guide to Corporate Culture* in 2013 and *FASTBREAK: The CEOs Guide to Strategy Execution* in 2014. I guess I'm a slow learner since I am making new discoveries about leadership, culture and performance every day, mostly thanks to my clients and our many late evening discussions over a Single Malt Scotch, or two.

This book is a culmination of my most recent research and thinking about the core principles which build, drive, sustain and reshape corporate culture.

 Culture rules! And Culture has rules!

Just what is

Corporate Culture?

 Corporate Culture is like the water in a fish tank.
Let it go foul and everything suffers.

Corporate culture is analogous to the DNA of a company. DNA determines much of who we are as humans. Culture influences how those inside a company work and behave. Corporate Culture is that unique combination of behaviors, beliefs, assumptions and business processes (formal and informal) that over time have become the *"habitual"* or *"default"* approach management and employees use in solving business problems and interacting with peers, customers, clients and suppliers.

In humans and in organizations alike, habitual or default behaviors are so commonplace as to be nearly invisible. A newly hired executive or hourly employee can see the culture very clearly because everything is new to them, but the newness wears off quickly and soon the culture is taken for granted as *"the way we do things"*. The ubiquity of expressions like *"it is what it is"* and *"it's just our culture"* show how things are taken for granted inside most companies.

Throughout this book I will use the term **corporate culture**, or just plain **culture**. There are numerous other terms often used, such as organizational health, and the classical academic term **organization culture**. While the academics may take issue to my lumping of these various terms under the umbrella of culture, this is not an academic review but a practical guide book to help those leading and working in organizations better understand and shape their corporate culture. As one pragmatic CEO told me: *"Spare me the academic mumbo jumbo and consultant gobbledygook. Give me something I can use to improve my business and the lives of my employees!"*

As far as I can tell, the first real mention of corporate culture in a business context comes from the pioneering work of Elliott Jaques (1917–2003), a Canadian psychoanalyst and organizational psychologist who studied the human dynamics within a manufacturing factory, with a particular emphasis on layers of management and how people behaved in carrying out duties and work orders from above. This first mention of culture appeared in his 1951 book *The Changing Culture of a Factory: A Study of Authority and Participation in an Industrial Setting*,[9] and Jaques' definition remains one of the most succinct and all-encompassing:

 The culture of the factory is its customary and traditional way of thinking and of doing things, which is shared to a greater or lesser extent by all its members, and which new members must learn, and at least partially accept, in order to be accepted into service in the firm. [It] consists of the means or techniques which lie at the disposal of the individual for handling his relationships, and upon which he depends for making his way among, and with, other members and groups.

Scores of academics and business psychologists began to research and write about corporate culture after 1951, but most studies were based on either observational or anecdotal data. It was not until 1992 that Harvard professors John P. Kotter and James L. Heskett made one of the first real connections between the soft concept of culture and the hard economic realities of business performance metrics in their book, *Corporate Culture and Performance*.[10] Kotter and Heskett studied over 200 firms, including Hewlett-Packard, Xerox, ICI and Nissan, and concluded that adaptive cultures—those that are flexible enough to evolve with changing market conditions—tended to perform better economically than non-adaptive cultures.

By the mid-90s, the concept of corporate culture had become firmly established in the lexicon of international business and began to be taught in MBA courses as well as Advanced Executive Education workshops at top business schools like Harvard, MIT and INSEAD. It was around this time that the consulting profession discovered the growing and lucrative market for culture change projects and culture surveys, and the literature exploded with articles, opinion pieces, courses, trainings, books, studies and even videos on corporate culture. This is when consultants, academics and high-profile senior executives began to put forth their various definitions of corporate culture.

The following are just a sampling of the many definitions of corporate (organizational) culture:

- The way we do things around here!

- Corporate Culture: those hard-to-change values that spell success or failure.

- Organization Culture: a pattern of shared basic assumptions learned by a group as it solved its problems of external adaptation and internal integration, which has worked well enough to be considered valid and, therefore, taught to new members as the correct way to perceive, think and feel in relation to those problems. [11]

- Culture is the collective programming of the human mind that distinguishes the members of one human group from those of another. Culture in this sense is a system of collectively held values. ~Geert Hofstede [12]

- The shared norms and expectations that govern the way people approach their work and interact with each other. Such norms and expectations shape how organizational members believe they are expected to behave in order to fit in, get things done, and at times simply survive. [13]

- Culture is to the organization what character and personality are to the individual. ~Joe Tye

- Culture is the organization's immune system. ~Michael Watkins

- Culture is an unwritten set of ground-rules on what is acceptable and what is not.

Culture and Business Value

 Competitors can buy tangible assets, but they can't buy culture.
~Herb Kelleher

In their 2016 Global Human Capital Trends survey, Deloitte reports that 82 percent of those interviewed believe culture to be a potential competitive advantage.[14] Duke University recently interviewed approximately 1,900 CEOs and CFOs from companies representing 20% of the total US Market Value to determine what those in business leadership positions considered the top drivers of economic market value.[15] Surprisingly, corporate culture came out as the top business value driver, closely followed by the strategic plan and the operating plan.

Most Important Business **VALUE** Drivers
(Duke University Research Study 2016: 1900 CEOs and CFOs)

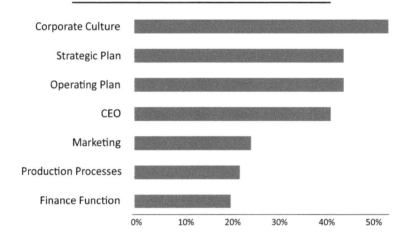

Okay, so a large number of executives believe culture has an impact on performance, but what's the evidence? Is there a tangible relationship between corporate culture and financial performance? There seems to be.

McKinsey research has found that companies with strong performance cultures have an 11 percent higher annual total return to shareholders (TRS) and 5.2 percent higher return on investment capital (ROIC) than those with weak performance cultures.[16]

In companies where traditional performance improvement programs were compared with those that added culture change approaches as well, the business impact of combined performance improvement and culture change delivered significantly greater business results.[17]

Business impact of performance culture interventions

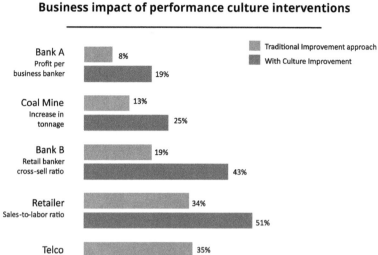

At the business operating level, the landmark longitudinal study in the late 1990s by the department store chain Sears found that a 5-point increase in its internal culture survey correlated to a 1.3-point improvement in customer satisfaction, which in turn correlated to a $250 million increase in revenue across all stores.[18] Between 1992 and 2000, Sears CEO and culture believer Arthur Martinez engineered a stunning turnaround and return to profitability by focusing on the customer experience. It's a shame that successive CEOs didn't take culture as seriously as Martinez, instead believing that retail success is more about price and selection than the customer experience.

Sears is now a shadow of its former self; the result of cost cutting, layoffs, selling off brands and closing stores. In 2005 Sears was bought by Kmart, but even with successive infusions of cash, remains on a downward spiral. What is ironic is that long before the Internet and its growing domination of retail sales, Sears was the world leader in catalog retail sales. In essence, Sears was an early 20th Century version of Amazon.

A study by Professor Eric Flamholtz on the 18 operating divisions of one company convincingly shows that differences in corporate culture can account for as much as 46% of EBIT.[19] While there is currently no line item on most balance sheets for corporate culture, there is a growing agreement that culture is a significant driver of business economic value.

For individuals, character is destiny.
For companies, culture is destiny. ~Tony Hsieh, Zappos

Culture is an Outcome

Most writing on corporate culture takes a behavioral psychology approach in suggesting that changing employee behaviors will result in a change in culture. From a strictly business perspective, however, we can observe that certain habitual behaviors exhibited by employees at all levels are actually the outcome of a certain set of culture drivers. Behaviors are not the culture, but the outcome of a corporate culture system.

If you are trying to change culture and human behavior through training, culture workshops, coaching and other forms of business psychology interventions without also changing the other numerous drivers of culture, you are wasting time and money.

 *Every culture is perfectly aligned with the **real** purpose of the business, not the stated purpose. The trouble is, the market and employees may not support that purpose.*

In a typical culture change scenario, the CEO and Vice President of Stores decide that the behaviors on the sales floor needs to shift to better focus on the customer and the customer shopping experience. Front-line employees need better skills and new ways of behaving in line with a more customer-centric culture, so a series of culture change workshops are developed for store staff. This is a complex and costly operation, in which service levels and sales revenue can drop while employees are sent away for training. Nevertheless, the VP is committed, and the plan rolls out over a 6-month period in all stores.

The training is highly interactive, the case studies are believable, and the facilitators engaging and knowledgeable about the day-to-day life of a retail sales person. End-of-workshop evaluations are high and a huge surge of positive energy is released. Posters from the workshops show up in all the staff lounges, the administrative offices and other non-customer-facing areas. For the next several weeks, the customer experience is transformed by interactions with willing and helpful staff, and everyone is upbeat. Morale and employee engagement stay high when first quarter same-store sales are found to have increased compared to the last year, and there is even a monthly newsletter devoted to the customer service principles taught in the workshop.

Job done! The culture has been changed. Well, not quite.

Inevitably, second quarter same-store sales drop back to previous levels, employee engagement surveys are now lower than before, and customer complaints and staff turnover increase. It is quickly determined that the training was substandard and before long there are several new faces in the training department, as well as a new VP of Stores.

The sad fact is the desired staff behaviors and store culture changes don't last. Why the regression? It's not because of poor training design, but because management fails to understand that behaviors are not the corporate culture, but are the outcomes of the corporate culture system. Several aspects of the overall corporate culture within this particular retail company didn't change, nor were they even recognized as strong drivers of the poor service culture.

Let me describe to you the corporate culture system of this particular retailer and a few of the culture drivers that result in poor customer service at the store level. This retail company believed strongly in the importance of merchandising, which was at the heart of its business model. While the CEO ran retail operations, the Chairman was in charge of merchandising. In this culture, merchandising was the most important function, and the Buyers the most powerful and feared people in the company. Even during weekly senior executive meetings, the Chairman and Senior Buyers took control and most of the discussions were about fashion trends, buying patterns, sales trends, budgets and stock levels. Customer service and corporate culture almost never appeared on the agenda.

To be successful and meet or exceed their sales quotas and to keep up with shifting customer preferences and trends, a Buyer needed to know the exact level of his or her stock across all stores, and would always insist their merchandise be unloaded, stocked, and replenished first. This job fell to the store sales staff, who were responsible for both customer service and stocking. It was not uncommon for Senior Buyers to call and text to demand a stock check several times throughout the day. The Store Manager would dutifully pass these requests to the sales staff, who knew that orders coming from the Senior Buyers were to take precedence over any other activities.

It is obvious in this example that merchandising procedures and processes were the major drivers of the culture in the stores. Exhausted sales staff couldn't simultaneously please the buyers while providing the level of service customers expected, and something had to give. Unfortunately for the customers, it was service. Unfortunately for the company, it was the brand's image and eventually its stock price. This is what usually happens when the real corporate culture drivers of employee behavior are poorly understood. The only winner in this scenario is the competition.

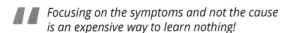 *Focusing on the symptoms and not the cause is an expensive way to learn nothing!*

A New Understanding:

Corporate Culture as a Business System

 Systems are the essential building blocks of every successful business. ~Ron Carroll

When the culture consultant or business psychologist thinks about a company or organization, they usually focus on values, beliefs and workplace behaviors. Perhaps accurate, but definitely not the entire picture. In my mind, this approach is akin to looking at the world through a straw and only seeing a narrow piece of the entire landscape.

A successful business strategy is the result of choices about pricing, product design, customer demand, supply chain sustainability and marketing. Clever pricing alone cannot deliver competitive advantage, since customers also care about quality, product safety, design, the shopping experience and numerous other requirements. To say the least, a winning competitive strategy requires integrating all elements and functions of the company into the strategic business system.

The same is true for corporate culture. Corporate culture reflects the complex interactions between business structures, policies and people. These interrelated culture drivers form an end-to-end system, the corporate culture system. Although leadership behaviors and values are some of the most written and talked about drivers of corporate culture, those two ingredients alone are insufficient to create a successful corporate culture.

Before embarking on an attempt to change or reshape corporate culture, senior executive teams must understand the drivers and building blocks of their own unique corporate culture. Every company has a unique set of drivers, even if they are in the same industry.

An in-depth understanding of corporate culture requires seeing it as an end-to-end business process, which begins with the major drivers of culture and ends with business performance outcomes. By constructing an end-to-end process map and then stepping back, it is much easier to see the many culture drivers that exist. With this knowledge, a savvy leadership team can use their culture-as-a-system process map to better align people and behaviors with their business model and strategic objectives.

 If you can't describe what you are doing as a process, you don't know what you are doing. ~W. Edwards Deming

Seeing culture as a business system allows one to better understand not only the drivers of culture but more importantly where they reside in the company. Those familiar with extended supply chains will understand the value of mapping how materials flow from multiple suppliers in diverse locations into the company warehouse, onto the manufacturing floor and into the final product. A corporate culture system map can also be viewed as an end-to-end flow process. These culture drivers provide the meaning and context for what we see as cultural behaviors and habitual work practices which are often described by current employees as *"how we do things around here"*.

The Corporate Culture System

Below is a high level generic corporate culture system map. As you can see, the various external and internal drivers interact with established internal business practices and human social systems to build and sustain a unique corporate culture, which impacts the ability of the company to deliver on its business performance objectives.

Corporate Culture End-to-End System

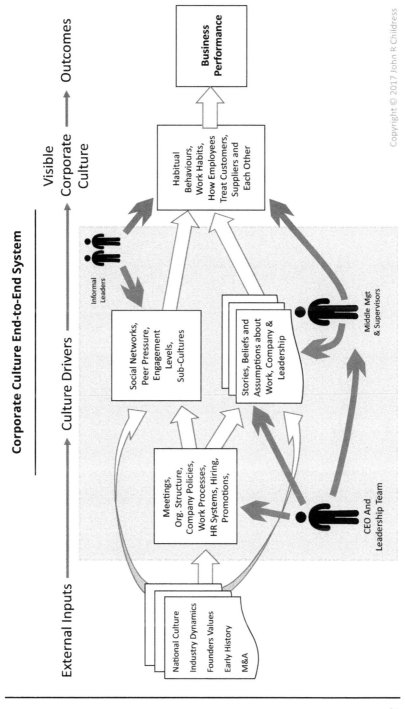

Several useful insights emerge when corporate culture is viewed as a business system. With this point of view, not only are the real drivers that build and sustain the culture more easily identified and clearly defined, but a systems map of culture also makes it possible to find the most effective levers for culture change.

 A good hacker tries first to understand the entire system and then focuses his efforts on the weakest steps

For example, Informal Leaders, those individuals whom large numbers of employees tend to respect and listen to, and who often provide important advice to new hires about how to survive in the company and who to trust, have a huge influence on the actual culture. Informal leaders are key influencers in any business transformation and culture change process. In most views of culture, they are invisible. Likewise, the impact of Founder Values and Early Company History are often overlooked as key drivers behind how the company is organized and assumptions about work and life inside the company.

A systems view of culture is also useful in understanding that the various drivers of the culture are not all of equal strength in determining the nature of an organization's culture. In fact, each driver has a different weighting in terms of its impact on the culture. This is a factor that the majority of culture assessments on the market tend to ignore, believing instead that all factors have equal importance in determining the culture.

 A bad system will defeat a good employee every time.
~W. Edwards Deming

The Drivers That Build and Sustain Corporate Culture

The chart below shows the relative strengths of the key internal and external drivers of corporate culture in most companies. As we further explore the 10 Core Principles of corporate culture, you will gain a better understanding of why some drivers have more impact on shaping culture than others, and how they often interact to produce a specific company culture.

Relative Strengths of Culture Drivers

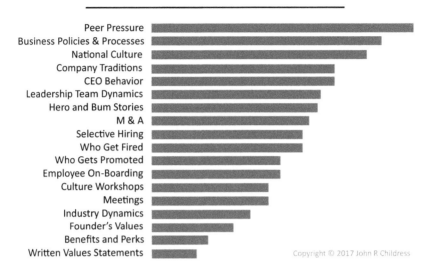

Peer Pressure
Business Policies & Processes
National Culture
Company Traditions
CEO Behavior
Leadership Team Dynamics
Hero and Bum Stories
M & A
Selective Hiring
Who Get Fired
Who Gets Promoted
Employee On-Boarding
Culture Workshops
Meetings
Industry Dynamics
Founder's Values
Benefits and Perks
Written Values Statements

The most important culture driver is **Peer Pressure**, a constant and powerful, yet nearly invisible shaper of the culture. Organizations may be shown as hierarchies on organization charts, but they are actually a complex web of social networks and subcultures, where the innate human need to belong and fit in with the group is extremely strong. Peer pressure is the enforcer of the informal ground rules within the subcultures and the company as a whole. It is also the place where rumors about upper management or business decisions spread, and gain credibility. When the behavior of the CEO or a senior executive is out of alignment with the stated values, the stories gain momentum through peer to peer discussions, and often get twisted to fit the beliefs of the informal leaders. On the other hand, peer pressure can be a highly positive force in the culture when respected subculture leaders help drive company values and desired behaviors.

The second most powerful drivers of organizational culture are **Policies & Processes**, which includes both company policies and internal business processes. These form an organizational technology and represent the collection of rules, methods and processes used by management to organize and align employees for the accomplishment of business objectives. Company policies and procedures have an enormous impact on employee attitudes and actions in the day-to-day workplace and are key builders and drivers of corporate culture. Some business policies and processes, such as performance reviews, office space design and compensation, dramatically impact how people behave inside an organization. The annual budgeting process is notorious for instilling a rigid set of unwritten rules about what is important. In many companies, obsession with internal budgets creates a culture of inward focus. Instead of looking outward at market needs, advancing technologies, customer expectations or competitor movements, a great deal of time is spent in meetings analyzing, forecasting, recasting, cutting and defending functional budgets.

The seminal work of Geert Hofstede [12] in describing how **National Culture** determines employee beliefs and behaviors is too often overlooked in the popular writing about corporate culture. A German automaker can have a very different culture from an American automaker, as is evidenced in the disastrous so called *"merger of equals"* between Daimler-Benz and Chrysler in 1998. National cultures play a large part in the failure of many companies trying to establish operations in other countries and regions.

Company Traditions can be extremely strong, although they are often overlooked by new CEOs from the outside as they strive to improve performance. However, when the new strategies or changes go against strong company habits and beliefs, they often meet with considerable resistance. For many organizations, a company's history and traditions are a strong part of the current culture. The legacy history and traditions of Coca-Cola is an enormous driver of pride and belief in the product; so much so that the company has dedicated an enormous amount of money and effort in celebrating its heritage. There is even a World of Coke museum in Atlanta. Legacy traditions are also known to lead to surprising priorities, like how Steve Jobs' early fascination with calligraphy provided a strong foundation for Apple's fixation with aesthetic and functional product design. In some companies, the 30-minute, early Monday morning staff meeting has become so important that traveling executives create time to dial in so as not to miss out on important issues.

Many culture experts claim that **CEO Behavior** and **Leadership Team Dynamics** are the strongest culture drivers. This may be true when a company is small and the CEO knows everyone and is actively involved with the product, customers and employees. However, as a company grows larger and becomes publically traded or global in scope, the physical impact of the CEO on the culture is drastically reduced, with most of their time taken up meeting with the press and analysts, or internal meetings about strategy, costs and product problems. To most employees in a large company, the CEO and senior team are nearly invisible. Yet even if they aren't visible to all employees, the shadow cast by their behaviors reaches down to all employees through the power of peer to peer discussions. And these stories about leadership behavior are often greatly magnified, which can be good news or bad news.

The positive stories and leadership shadow of Sam Walton are still alive inside Walmart. The stories of excessive perks and rude behavior of senior executives in some investment banks also spreads quickly, with a definite impact on employee respect and trust for management. Far too often, the CEO and senior leaders are clueless about the shadows they cast and the impact of their behavior on the culture. And in a culture of mistrust and cynicism, the impact of the CEO and leadership team intent on positive change can actually be blunted by the internal corporate culture.[20]

Hero and Bum Stories are where the culture comes alive for new employees. Forget the 50-page on-line handbook or the required videos about compliance and company history. A number of hero and bum stories are widely circulated and repeated when employees gather at lunch or around the espresso machine. Stories of what actions led to firings, who did something extraordinary for a customer, and who is the best manager to work for tend to imprint company culture into the hearts and minds of employees.

Mergers and Acquisitions often fail to deliver on the expected deal synergies and outcomes due to culture clash. Few M&A advisors take into account cultural differences, relying instead on balance sheet optimization and strategic fit to make the marriage work. When Textron Systems acquired AAI a culture assessment pointed out significant differences in many of the leadership and HR practices which could have slowed down the integration process had not Textron leadership revised their integration plan to take these cultural differences into account.

 The results from the culture integration assessment took me by surprise. It pointed out, in a very quantitative and visual way, the areas we had overlooked in our traditional integration assessment. But it didn't take us long to plug this new information into our plans.
~Ellen Lord, former CEO, Textron Systems Companies

Selective Hiring, **Who Gets Fired** and **Who Gets Promoted** are significant culture drivers. Often management has an unconscious positive bias towards *"people like us"*, that is those with similar resumes and job experiences. And if you went to the same University or are from one of the top schools, you are automatically a favored candidate. It is not uncommon to hire people from the CEO's former company. And everyone in the company watches carefully who gets promoted and who gets fired and quickly interpret these actions as clues for advancement and survival. These form a large part of the informal ground rules that everyone knows, except the senior leaders, of course. That's why the greatest firms in the world have some of the most stringent recruiting policies.

Employee On-Boarding is a big factor in whether or not new employees get indoctrinated into the desired company culture. Unless there is a robust on-boarding process, new employees will bring their old company culture with them as their default behavior, along with attitudes about work which may be counter to the values and behaviors required at the new company. Companies that understand the importance of corporate culture have rigorous new employee on-boarding processes, sometimes a week long, which help establish accepted ways of working inside the company and prove highly useful in gaining alignment between employees and organizational objectives.

Culture Workshops, the main deliverable of most culture consultancies, can be strong drivers towards imbedding behaviors and beliefs into the corporate culture. Culture change workshops can build energy, enthusiasm and optimism, and add energy and emotion to an ongoing cultural change program. They are especially impactful when in combination with changes in other culture drivers such as company policies and processes. In too many cases, employees become disillusioned when returning to the workplace soon after the workshop ends only to find the same old policies and practices, the same old supervisor behaviors, the same old management attitudes, and little reinforcement of the workshop concepts.

Meetings are an almost perfect microcosm of company culture. Dozens of meetings occur at every level every day and it is here that the "real culture" is on display. Whether the meetings are well organized or loose and rambling, whether the chairperson dominates or there is equal participation, whether the major focus is on costs or on customers, or whether meetings look to place blame or find solutions, they are a place where corporate culture is reinforced and sustained on a daily level.

Every corporate culture is influenced and shaped by its particular **Industry Dynamics**. For example, the retail industry values speed, risk-taking and quick changes based on customer buying patterns. Nothing is exempt from change. Those who thrive and survive in this culture tend to display high energy, empathy towards customers and quick decision making skills. High tech companies, on the other hand, tend to favor those with an engineering mindset and in many cases are highly skewed towards young males, with women being reluctantly included. And aerospace companies make decisions slowly and after extensive analysis and study since the product development cycles are long and supply chains complex. Those with high analytical skills tend to thrive in this industry, which on the other hand does not always put a premium on communications skills.

Founder's Values and beliefs about how a business should be run often become baked into the early business model and internal policies and procedures. Sam Walton's strong beliefs about keeping costs down, delivering value to customers, and the importance of gathering data on customer buying patterns formed a large part of the success of Wal-Mart in its early years. Founder values and beliefs are a major driver in the early stages of a business, but as a company grows and expands and brings in new leadership, few organizations continue to drive and reinforce founder stories and values, opting instead to follow new trends, try to match their competitors, and satisfy the quarterly demands of Wall Street. A good example is the continued deterioration of the British Airways brand aa it continues to cut costs, charge for once free services, and homogenize the customer experience to match other airlines.

Some of the weakest culture drivers are the **Benefits and Perks** and **Written Values Statements**. Many articles showcasing the characteristics of great workplaces discuss company benefits and perks, such as Friday beer blasts, foosball tables and bean bags, making it seem easy for any company to build a culture by copying these rituals. Often, these perks have little or no impact on how work gets done and while they may attract new employees, are not strong drivers of retention.

Written Values Statements, on the other hand, rarely have any impact at all. The Enron corporate values of Respect, Integrity, Communications and Excellence, were summarily ignored by its leaders in the quest for profit and share price growth. And when a new CEO creates a revised set of "company values", employees quickly learn the effort is more about PR and *"optics"* than guidelines for day-to-day work behaviors. For company values to become strong culture drivers, they need to be imbedded in all parts of the business, not just brochures or Annual Reports.[21]

The above mentioned culture drivers interact inside the corporate culture system to mold and sustain employee behaviors and beliefs about the company, its leaders and products. The failure of many culture change initiatives often comes down to the change program focusing on only a few, highly visible culture drivers and missing out on one or more of the strongest and most influential. When the organizational culture system is properly aligned with the strategic business objectives and the current economic climate, corporate culture is a powerful driver of positive business outcomes and high levels of employee engagement.

As we explore the 10 Core Principles of Corporate Culture in the next few chapters, the relative weighting of the many culture drivers mentioned above will become clearer. Keeping in mind that some culture levers tend to be more powerful than others will help in understanding how culture can become a powerful business tool for improved performance.

 Wells Fargo designed a system that produced bad behavior. When you find that out, you gotta do something about it, and the big mistake was they didn't do something about it.
~Warren Buffet

Section One

The 10 Core Principles of Corporate Culture

The 10 Core Principles of Corporate Culture

> **❝❝** *Policies are many, Principles are few,*
> *Policies will change, Principles never do. ~ John C. Maxwell*

In 1687, Isaac Newton published his *Philosophiæ Naturalis Principia Mathematica*. The *Principia* includes Newton's laws of motion, the foundation of classical mechanics, Newton's law of universal gravitation, and a derivation of Kepler's laws of planetary motion. Newton's *Principia* is universally regarded as one of the most important works in the history of science.

The fundamental principles laid out by Newton formed the foundation for a revolution in science and the beginning of modern physics. He even invented a form of mathematics we now know as calculus. Much of the progress we have today in engineering, physics, space travel, GPS and modern living are solidly based on Newton's principles.

Core principles can be relied upon to be true, to work, to produce the expected results, time and time again. Many business and management maxims are in reality theories, based more on anecdotes, correlations and individual beliefs than core principles. Everywhere we look in the management and business literature about leadership there are theories, correlations, fables and examples, but very few fundamental core principles that, if followed, repeatedly produce great leadership.

The same is true of corporate culture. Fundamental core principles of corporate culture exist, and they are highly useful for predictably understanding, guiding and reshaping organizational cultures to align with business strategy. These principles are not new, nor are they as complex as rocket science, and yet in few instances are they actually applied with focus, commitment, and discipline in an integrated manner.

As I speak about corporate culture to audiences large and small, and in my advisory work with CEOs and senior leadership teams, I often use the following 10 Core Principles as we chart a course together for sustainable competitive advantage and a well-run business. These core principles are essential for understanding how a corporate culture system operates, how it can be changed, and how it can affect a company's performance.

- o   Principle One: Every Organization Has a Culture
- o   Principle Two: Culture Impacts Performance
- o   Principle Three: Culture Can Be a Significant Business Risk
- o   Principle Four: Culture Works on Human Logic, Not Business Logic
- o   Principle Five: Organizations are Shadows of Their Leaders
- o   Principle Six: Cultural Drift
- o   Principle Seven: Policies Drive Culture More Than We Realize.
- o   Principle Eight: You Get the Culture You Ignore
- o   Principle Nine: There Is No Perfect Corporate Culture
- o   Principle Ten: Leaders and Employees Change Cultures, Not Consultants

Together, these ten principles form a coherent picture of the corporate culture system. Each individual principle is important, yet not sufficient in and of itself, much like the various pieces of a jigsaw puzzle. These 10 principles, taken together and each given its proper weighting in light of company strategy and market dynamics, provide a useful understanding of the business and human impact of corporate culture. And more importantly, how to leverage culture for improved business success.

 There are three constants in life...
change, choice and principles. ~Stephen Covey

Principle One:

Every Organization Has a Culture

❝ Every organization exhibits a culture. The departments within the organization have a culture. Anytime people work together for an extended period of time, a culture is formed. It's the force that guides and directs how people will interact with one another and deal with those beyond their group.[22]
~John Schultz

Large or small, start-up or mature, commercial or government, every organization has a culture. A corporate culture is either designed from the beginning or left to develop by default. Either way, you will have a corporate culture.

Stop and reflect for a moment. Remember your first week in your current company? Sure you were excited about the new challenge and the opportunities for learning and proving yourself. But also think about how different it was. The offices and desks may look the same, the cubicles similar, the computers and other equipment recognizable, but how people think and act, their beliefs about the company and management, the stories they tell about the company, the degree of optimism or pessimism, the frequency of face-to-face discussions versus email blasts. Everything was different.

To many new employees, whether senior executive, front line worker or part-time call center staff, the way things work in their new company is often very different from their previous company. New hires can see and feel a company's culture at every turn. But for those who have worked in the company for several months or years, cultural myopia sets in and the corporate culture becomes so ubiquitous and commonplace as to be nearly invisible. When cultural myopia sets in, no amount of culture audits or management consultant PowerPoints will make it come alive. I firmly believe that culture is tangible and must be experienced in order for employees to see its real business meaning and value.

A while ago I organized a field trip for the senior executives and team leads of an industrial products manufacturing company. They were having a difficult time getting their waste reduction and quality improvement programs implemented. The company spent thousands of dollars and hundreds of man-hours on training. They re-engineered the layout of the manufacturing areas in line with Lean Principles, but were still plagued with quality problems and costly waste in both materials and time.

The field trip was to a company with a totally different corporate culture than my client. I had mentioned this company during several workshops with my client, but somehow the team always came back with excuses like *"yeah, but we're different"* and *"our union is the real problem"*. My client couldn't accept that such a nebulous concept as corporate culture could be the real culprit.

When we arrived at the company the first order of business was a tour of the factory. Like my client's factory, it was clean, it had daily schedule boards, and tac-time clocks. Noting earth shattering. They did, however, notice a different vibe or buzz among the employees, and a lot more smiles. Most of the visitors passed it off as *"being on their best behavior for the guests"*.

After lunch we gathered in the conference room, our team and theirs. To focus the discussion away from technical or equipment issues and towards culture, I asked the host team what it was like to work in their company. Everybody from the senior executives to the work team leaders talked about the trust they put in employees to solve problems rather than escalate them, the honest feedback, the appreciation for jobs well done, and the way all employees were brought into the decision making process for changes that would affect them, such as layout, equipment purchases, and work schedules. The team spoke enthusiastically about how they often invited customers in to talk about quality issues and product suggestions. Although both companies were in manufacturing and drew employees from the same surrounding region, it soon became obvious the two cultures were completely different.

Weeks afterwards the visiting team still talked about the culture they experienced, constantly comparing it with their own. Needless to say, their commitment to reshaping culture gained momentum and the next several quarters saw a steady improvement in quality, waste and overall employee engagement.

 Experience isn't the best teacher, it's the only teacher.
~Dr. Albert Schweitzer

A management team clueless about culture runs the risk of missing a valuable early warning mechanism for catching potential business productivity and revenue problems before they materialize. The diagram below describes the "knock-on effect" of culture on performance and how understanding the multiple culture drivers can act as an early warning system. Recognizing a downturn in culture or employee engagement early provides valuable time for leadership to develop countermeasures before productivity and profitability decline.

Culture As An Early Warning System

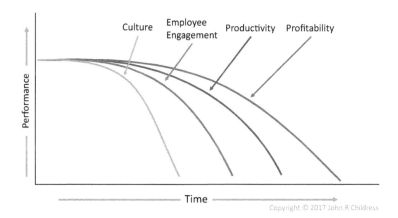

 An organization that waits for a significant downturn in financial measures such as growth and profit to signal the need for change is doomed to fail. ~James Heskett

For many companies, it is only during a crisis that culture becomes highly visible and real, and *"the way we do things around here"* becomes evident.

When confronted with the facts about the Volkswagen emissions fraud, CEO Martin Winterkorn vehemently denied the issue, only later as more and more evidence was presented and the public outcry grew did he admit to the fraud and the resulting cover-up. Winterkorn denied the issue because a culture of *"shoot the messenger"*, combined with an insistence on looking perfect at all costs, led to his avoidance of acknowledging anything that was out of the norm or below the stated goals. From the CEO on down everyone was caught up in the Volkswagen culture. The positive side of this results-obsessed culture helped them surpass Toyota to become the largest car company in the world. But the results-obsessed, no-bad-news culture eventually cost upwards of $20 billion in fines and a massive hit to their market valuation and overall brand reputation, which may never recover.[23]

 *If you don't manage your culture,
it will manage you.*

One way to understand the effects of corporate culture in black and white is to take a look at medical claims, healthcare premiums, accident rates, turnover, absenteeism, errors and defects. These are some of the business metrics (and human costs) attributable to workplace culture.

Another way to understand culture is to see it as internal bureaucracy. Recently, Gary Hamel, visiting professor at London Business School, has focused his research and unique critical thinking skills on reducing organizational bureaucracy, which he estimates costs the U.S. economy more than $3 trillion in lost economic output per year.[24] Hamel estimates that across the 32 OECD countries, the cost of excess bureaucracy could be as high as $9 trillion. Hamel suggests that bureaucracy is a direct reflection of the culture of the organization, and it encompasses many of the elements that make up the corporate culture system.

Hamel lists 7 categories of culture-related costs: Bloat, friction, insularity, disempowerment, risk aversion, inertia and politics. He also states that upending cultural norms isn't easy, saying that *"it takes courage, a dose of righteous indignation, and, perhaps most critical, data. People pay attention to things that can be measured"*. He then goes on to provide a survey/assessment tool to determine the impact of bureaucracy, which is actually a good proxy for a beginning culture assessment.

Most academics believe that the best way to see your company's culture is to measure it with a culture assessment or diagnostic survey. I am not a great fan of traditional culture assessment tools since in most cases they ask standardized questions, are built on averages, fail to take into account subcultures, are developed using correlative data rather than cause and effect, and treat all culture drives as having the same weight in determining culture. While two of the most useful culture survey tools on the market are the Denison Culture Assessment and the McKinsey Organization Health Index, there are other ways to understand the strengths and weaknesses of your culture and the critical drivers and levers for change.

<u>Why</u> Beats <u>What</u> or <u>How</u> Every Time

Instead of large expensive culture surveys, one of my favorite methods of understanding a corporate culture is to ask executives and employees to list what it's like to work here; the good news and the bad news. What will come out is a list of positives and negatives. Once you have this list, eliminate the redundant ones and with each one left, use the 5-Why process to get to the root cause.[25] For example, if employees say that *"it's a good place to develop useful skills"*, convene a focus group from different levels and start the 5-Why process. What you will normally find after several sessions, is a particular policy, a person or a set of company activities that drive and sustain that aspect of the culture. The same will be true of negative comments. In short order you will have uncovered a great deal about how your corporate culture really operates and the drivers that impact productivity, morale, engagement, customer experience and financial performance.

 The only purpose for me, in building a company, is so that that company can make products. One is a means to the other. Over a period of time, you realize that building a very strong company and a very strong foundation of talent and culture in a company is essential to making great products. ~Steve Jobs

Whether consciously or unconsciously, every culture develops to fulfil a purpose. That purpose may be as simple as make a profit at all costs, to as noble and far-reaching as change the way passengers experience air travel. With this insight, it is easy to see that every culture is perfectly aligned with its real purpose. And in many cases, the problem is not with the culture or the people in the company, but with the overall purpose of the company in the first place.

Continental Airlines in the mid-1990s was an unhealthy amalgamation built from 7 previous airline mergers with a simple purpose, run cheap and make money. The run cheap they accomplished, but with their third bankruptcy just around the corner, they were definitely not making money. In an industry where customers have choice, poor service, late arrivals and lost baggage are not a winning business model.[26]

When Gordon Bethune took over as CEO of nearly bankrupt Continental Airlines in 1994 he asked a lot of Why questions. One such set of Why questions had to do with the treatment of customers by ticketing and check-in staff. Continental had the highest number of customer complaints on the monthly Department of Transportation airline performance statistics. In addition, customers hated to book with Continental because it was nearly impossible to make ticket changes without a near fight. And staff and ticket agents hated the negative association with the airline so much that they often removed their Continental logo badges when going to the grocery store to avoid negative comments.

 It's the old adage: You can make a pizza so cheap, nobody will eat it. You can make an airline so cheap, nobody will fly it. ~Gordon Bethune

Before Bethune started asking Why questions, the standard questions asked by Continental executives and managers was Who, as in *"who is to blame?"* The blame usually fell on the shoulders of the customer-facing counter staff, who would get grief from customers and double-grief from their managers. Bethune's regular asking Why helped him discover that the ultimate driver of a poor customer service culture was the thick and punitive Continental Rule Book, which had been continuously added to following successive airline mergers. It was a manual designed to keep the company from being taken advantage of by customers and it read like a legal document.

Bethune decided that in order to reshape the culture it was important for managers to trust their staff to use their best judgement to satisfy the customer and to protect the company. Many of the Continental employees had long tenures with the airline and knew what was fair and appropriate. To signal a true culture shift, Bethune held a ceremonial Rule Book burning in the parking lot of the Continental office complex in Houston and invited employees to participate. The onerous rules were replaced with a few common sense guidelines that employees helped develop.

These and other real changes in policies and operating procedures, as well as the removal of negative attitude managers at all levels moved Continental to profitability the very next year. In 1996 they were voted **Global Airline of the Year**, and delivered 16 straight quarters of record profits and reduced employee turnover by 45%. Continental stock price went from a low of $3.30 to $50 in 4 years.

 It all sounds almost silly, but the fact is that the only way to change a corporate culture is to just change it.
~Gordon Bethune

Principle Two:

Culture Impacts Performance

 Corporate culture is the only sustainable competitive advantage that is completely within the control of the entrepreneur. ~David Cummings, Co-Founder, Pardot

Adam Smith was a Scottish philosopher and a pioneer thinker in the area of the relationship between human behavior, politics and economics. His best known work, **The Wealth of Nations** (1776) is the first modern work of economics and his theories of how wealth is created and the forces behind economic prosperity are still influential today. His theories were based on a fundamental observation that normal human behavior is generally self-serving and people cooperate only when it is in their self-interest. And if all people behave similarly when it comes to business and financial dealings, then there is an *"invisible hand"* guiding the ups and downs of personal wealth and the prosperity of nations.

Adam Smith's term, the **Invisible Hand of the Market**, refers to the invisible market force that helps the supply and demand of goods and services in a free market reach equilibrium. According to Adam Smith, the process works naturally:

 Each individual strives to become wealthy attending only to his own gain, but to this end he must exchange what he owns or produces with others who sufficiently value what he has to offer; in this way, by division of labor and a free market, public interest is advanced.

Many of those in today's modern business world have somehow replaced the impact of human behavior on business performance with an almost maniacal focus on numbers, budgets, variances, costs, EBITDA and profit margins. We tend to manage with spreadsheets instead of managing and interacting with the people who actually produce the goods, buy the goods, and pay for the goods.

When asked why a small start-up could build Instagram while Kodak, which has now filed for bankruptcy protection, could not, Kodak board member Michael Hawley said: *"Cultural patterns are pretty hard to escape once you get sucked into them"*.[27] To paraphrase Adam Smith, the invisible hand of corporate culture has a great deal of influence on business performance.

 Think about the advantage of a place where talent wants to stay 25 years. Your turnover is lower, you don't have as many new people to train every year, you don't have as many mistakes. A seasoned workforce does a better job – and they cost you less money. ~David Rodriguez, CHRO, Marriott

While the ROI of culture may not be as directly measurable as the depreciation schedule on a piece of manufacturing equipment or a long-haul truck, culture is linked to much of the human activity in an organization which does impact costs and profits.[28] For example, the following are the knock-on cost impacts of corporate culture:

- o   Job satisfaction and employee *"ownership"* behaviors help in recruiting potential employees and providing suggestions for cost savings and innovative ways of doing things.

- o   Recruiting, hiring, and training costs are reduced when a large percentage of new hires come from referrals by current or former employees.

- o   New employees who join because they are attracted to the organization's values and culture improve retention rates and lower overall hiring costs.

- o   Greater retention rates keep wage levels more stable. High turnover tends to inflate wage scales for everyone, particularly at higher levels of management.

- o   Employees who remain longer provide the company benefits from higher productivity per dollar of compensation, or in economic terms, Returns-To-Labor.

o   Higher employee continuity leads to better relationships with customers, which in turn produces higher sales levels, customer retention and more word-of-mouth customer referrals, resulting in lower overall marketing costs.

Which comes first, organizational culture or performance? One of the few research studies on a causal link between culture and business success comes from data collected from 95 franchise automobile dealerships over a six-year period. The study determined that the measure of current culture consistently predicts future ratings of both customer satisfaction and car sales, but not the other way around.[29]

The Jaws of Culture

For years I have used a movie metaphor for the impact of culture on performance. Remember the Hollywood movie, Jaws, where a Great White Shark terrorizes a New England community, overcoming numerous attempts to banish or kill him? Nothing gets away from Jaws!

All business initiatives for change or improvement must first pass through what we have come to call the *"Jaws of Culture"*. Many business improvement initiatives, with extensive market research, followed by specific plans and milestones are regularly launched inside companies, but few make it through the *"Jaws of Culture"*.

A corporate culture whose default behaviors, mindsets and business practices are out of alignment with new initiatives being introduced, will quickly find ways, often covert, to block the required changes. Corporate Culture lies at the heart of most failed corporate initiatives, and in certain cases even corporate failures. On the other hand, a culture designed to be agile and receptive to change can actually help propel the uptake and delivery of new initiatives.

Look at the phenomenal success of Zappos.com; zero to $1 billion in revenue in less than 10 years. Or the tremendous economic value created by Ascend Communications, which grew from its founding in 1988 to being acquired in 1999 for $20 billion by Lucent Technologies in the largest such deal in the history of the data networking industry. Look at the long-term investing success of Berkshire Hathaway, Inc. and you will see a strong corporate culture based on shared beliefs and daily behaviors that breed further success.

 Our final advantage is the hard-to-duplicate culture that permeates Berkshire. And in businesses, culture counts.
~Warren Buffett

Strategy – Structure - Culture

The relationship between an organization's culture and business performance is easy to see with the understanding that strong

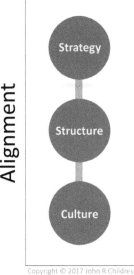

performance comes when strategy, structure and culture are aligned and interlinked. In top-performing companies, these three critical business elements are in alignment. Everyone knows where they are going (strategy), it's clear who does what in the organization (structure), and everyone understands the ground rules for working together and getting things done (culture).

In less turbulent times, when the pace of change was slower, organizations were able to maintain alignment between these three critical elements and as a result delivered predictable performance and long-term growth. The era of public monopolies, such as the Bell Telephone System and Television

Broadcasting are good examples of having the luxury of regulated stability to keep strategy, structure, and culture in alignment.

Sometimes the biggest obstacle to future success is past success. ~David Nadler

With the explosion of technology, globalization, aggressive new competition and shifting regulations, companies are often forced to develop and implement new strategies quickly. In order to adapt successfully, it is often necessary to reorganize in order to line up the organization to match the new strategy. The problem is, that's as far as most senior teams take it; thinking that improved performance should naturally follow. Because most CEOs and senior executives are often insulated from the real internal culture within their organization, it becomes difficult to see the link between culture and performance. It also becomes difficult to see when the existing culture is no longer aligned with the new demands of the business.

Many organizations get into trouble not because of a failed strategy, but because of a rigid culture.

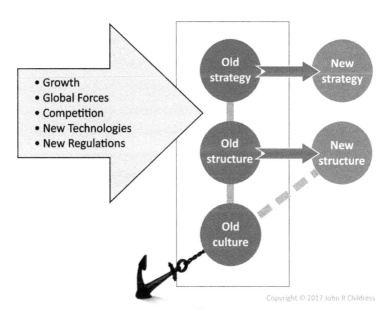

Unless there is work done to reshape corporate culture, the old culture can act as an anchor, slowing down and in some cases even stopping what might otherwise be an effective strategy execution. To fully implement a new strategy or to rebuild your organization to be effective in a changed world, it is also critical to reshape your corporate culture.

Corporate culture is also related to employee turnover, and turnover has a significant impact on business efficiency, customer service levels and costs. High turnover results in significant lost opportunity costs as well as direct costs of hiring and training.[30,31]

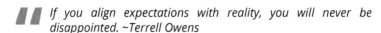 *If you align expectations with reality, you will never be disappointed. ~Terrell Owens*

Those who understand the relationship between culture and business performance also see culture as a competitive advantage.

Southwest Airlines, with a record of 44 consecutive years of positive net income, stands out in an industry plagued by losses and bankruptcy. The founder, Herb Kelleher, believes the Southwest culture, which is a combination of a low-cost business model, teamwork by all staff to reduce turnaround time, hiring for cultural fit, and an ethos of making flying fun, is their major competitive advantage.

Culture had a significant impact on the dramatic turnaround of Aetna, Inc.

 The single most important business reason to create a positive high-performance culture is the level and value of information leaders obtain when people are willing to discuss issues and problems. We know failures happen. When they occur, the leader needs to know what happened and what to do. In a negative culture people may try to cover mistakes and problems, and that undermines any real shot at performance improvement. In a positive and supportive culture, people will be more open to having fact-based discussions about problems, thereby allowing leaders to address those issues head on.
~Ron Williams, former Chairman and CEO, Aetna Inc.

One of the more insidious ways culture impacts business performance is through sacrosanct company policies. Several years ago a relatively new employee at a large British newspaper was curious why the papers were so big, so he asked one of the older executives. The reply came quickly. *"All quality newspapers are big; customers would not want it any other way".*

A few years later, a rival company – the *Independent* – halved the size of its newspaper, and saw a surge in circulation. Subsequently, many competitors followed, to similar effect. Yes, customers did want it.

The practice of large format newspapers began in London in 1712 because the English government started taxing newspapers by the number of pages they printed. So, publishers responded by printing their stories on so-called broadsheets, to minimize the number of sheets required and reduce their tax liability. This tax law was abolished in 1855 but newspapers continued printing on the impractically large sheets of paper for the next 150 years.

Usually established early in the formation of an organization, these ingrained policies, which govern *"how things should be done around here"*, impact every aspect of employee life, from the timing and content of expense reports and time cards, to pay scales and promotion requirements, to working times and vacation allotments, to the allocation of costs on the P&L. And company policy manuals are usually housed in multiple large binders.

And these are just the formal policies. In most companies the number of formal policies are dwarfed by the informal policies. Most of us recognize these informal rules of culture, such as the amount of openness and transparency of data shared, the power of a middle manager or supervisor, whether or not bad behavior is confronted or tolerated. In many ways, informal culture determines the quality of work, employee engagement levels and the ultimate ability of the company to deliver on its strategic objectives.

The example of the British newspapers above is just one of many where a policy formed in the 1700's to reduce printing costs because of taxation carried on long after the government policy was abolished in 1855. No one asked why they still printed broadsheet papers 150 years after the tax law was abolished, or if there was any real data for the preference of broadsheets over smaller paper sizes, or how much the company could reduce costs by going to a smaller format.

To those interested in competitive advantage and company performance, culture can be either an enabler or a barrier. Corporate culture is not just physical work behaviors, but also company mind-sets and habitual ways of thinking. And many successful and growing companies are built on a strong foundation and an adherence to their stated culture, which is often described as behaviors or truths or operating principles and are built in to every aspect of the organization.

Culture, Innovation and Performance

When Amazon began operations in 1994, few experts gave it a high probability of survival, especially with the company's focus on internet retail book sales and digital formats when everyone knew at the time that people with a passion for books liked browsing and handling the real thing. Amazon's business model of continually money-losing in the pursuit of growth seemed foolish, but what most didn't realize at the time is that throughout these early years Amazon was building a corporate culture obsessed with finding and delivering customer value, coupled with a drive for relentless innovation. That culture was fanned through data driven decisions and a maniacal focus on hiring to fit culture profiles. In those early money losing years a culture was taking shape that would be the foundation for what is now the largest global retailer by market value and a company with an estimated $19 billion in cash reserves.

Stephenie Landry, an Amazon operations executive, was obsessed with how to shorten delivery times for customers. She developed the idea of rushing goods to urban customers in one hour or less. But she didn't stop there. One hundred and eleven days later she oversaw the start of a new Amazon service, Prime Now, where *"a customer was able to get a Frozen doll on Amazon when they could not find one in all of New York City, and it was delivered to their house in 23 minutes".* As of April, 2017, Amazon's market cap was $439.8 billion, larger than the combined valuations of rival retailers Walmart, Costco, Target, Macy's and Kohl's.[32]

 My main job today? I work hard at helping to maintain the culture. ~Jeff Bezos

Principle Three:

Culture Can Be
A Significant Business Risk

> *Risk comes from not knowing what you are doing.*
> *~Warren Buffett*

> *Risk comes from not knowing what your culture is doing.*
> *~John R Childress*

An IED is an Improvised Explosive Device, or in simple terms, a homemade bomb; sometimes detonated by remote control using a cell phone and other times with pressure from a vehicle or even a footfall. IEDs are the weapon of choice for insurgents against a larger, better equipped military. IEDs kill and maim without directly engaging the enemy. They are inexpensive to build but can cause great havoc to a traditional army.

Corporate culture is very much like an IED. We all know that culture impacts business performance, either positively or negatively and a culture not in alignment with the strategy and goals of the company can actually derail otherwise excellent business initiatives. Yet while most culture experts talk about values, the role of leadership and try to measure corporate culture, I believe they are missing a hugely important element of corporate culture.

> *Culture can be a significant business risk.*

Just like an IED is a risk to people driving or walking along a road or shopping in a crowded marketplace, culture can be a risk to business performance and the lives and well-being of employees at all levels.

Culture as Risk

The weather in the Gulf of Mexico was calm on the evening of April 20th, 2010 when a gas blowout and subsequent explosion occurred on the Deepwater Horizon oil rig, situated about 41 miles (66 km) off the southeast coast of Louisiana. The result was the worst oil spill in history. Eleven people died in the explosion, and fire damaged the rig to the point where it sank the next day. Fortunately, 115 people were safely rescued, but over the next 87 days an estimated 4.9 million barrels (210 million US gallons) of oil spilled into the Gulf of Mexico before the well hole 5,100 feet below the surface was finally capped.

A loss-of-life disaster is every senior executive's worst nightmare. The culture at British Petroleum made it worse. In the early days of the accident, BP leadership downplayed the incident, and CEO Tony Hayward called the amount of oil *"relatively tiny in comparison with the very big ocean"*.[33] To this day, it is unclear whether Hayward was playing down the extent of the disaster on purpose, or if the lines of communication within BP were so poor that he really didn't know what was going on. Either way, Hayward rightly faced serious criticism after a press conference when he said he was just as affected by the spill as Gulf Coast residents and complained about the interruption to his sailboat racing activities, saying *"you know, I'd like to have my life back"*.[34]

The Deepwater Horizon catastrophe ultimately cost Tony Haywood his job. So far BP has spent over $40 billion in recovery costs, set asides and settlements, and the litigation costs will likely continue to rise for the next 10 years. Prior to the Deepwater Horizon accident, BP's share price had been steadily increasing, outperforming the FTSE 100 index. As a result of how it handled the accident, BP has been vilified by the press and business journalists the world over. The BP share price was immediately cut in half and has yet to recover to its pre-accident level.

Fundamentally, BP at the time was a company with a culture intensely focused on the bottom line, with the combination of exploration investments and cost control being paramount to improving share price performance. In 2011, a White House commission blamed the disaster on BP and its partners for a series of cost-cutting decisions and an insufficient safety system.[35] At the time of the accident, the Deepwater rig was over budget and behind on its production schedule, putting more pressure on BP managers to move faster and return a profit.

As the Deepwater Horizon incident demonstrates, corporate culture has a profound and real impact on the performance of a business. Every corporation has a culture, and culture is never neutral or benign. Culture either has a positive or negative impact on a company's ability to perform. The corporate culture of British Petroleum posed a significant risk to business, to performance, to the share price and to human life.

 From our own experience in advising companies that have experienced ethical lapses, we have observed that the single most important force for preventing fraud and other misconduct and withstanding regulatory scrutiny is your corporate culture. ~PWC 2016 CEO Success study [36]

What makes corporate culture a potential business risk? Two things really.

First, culture is evidenced by how people routinely and habitually behave in business situations, with each other, and what they believe to be important for personal success. In the case of the offshore oil and gas industry for example, strong subcultures exist among pipefitters, welders, drill crews, and other operationally intensive functions. Crew bosses, often with strong personalities and years of experience, oversee younger and less experienced workers eager to be the best, prove themselves in the eyes of their peers, and please the boss.

In such a situation, crew members can easily resort to shortcuts and potentially unsafe actions, reinforced by peer pressure to get the job done quickly and keep the boss off their backs. In testimony before the US Senate Committee on Energy and Natural Resources, MIT Professor Nancy Leveson identified corporate culture as the most critical element of safety in the Oil and Gas industry.[37]

A culture of strong departmental silos with little open respect and poor cross-functional communication played a large role in the 1979 Three Mile Island nuclear accident. The Japanese national culture of deference to authority combined with a strong hierarchical corporate culture was a factor in the recent 2011 Fukushima Nuclear Plant disaster. The disastrous safety record of Korean Airlines, ranked 49 out of 60 global airlines in the 2016 JACDEC Airline Safety Rankings, showcases the combination of a strong national culture of deference to seniors and saving face, combined with an airline corporate culture modelled on the military hierarchy model where the captain is always right.

From the time it went public in 1998, Blackberry took only 10 years to capture 50% market share in the US and over 20% of the global smartphone market. At one point, RIM, the parent company, was the world's most valuable technology company, known for innovation and meeting the needs of time-challenged business people with secure communications, mobile productivity and constant email access. Over time, bureaucracy and a culture of internal fiefdoms led to fewer and fewer new product innovations and multiple product launch delays to such a degree that just 5 years later it was on life support with less than 3% market share.

The second factor making corporate culture a significant business risk is the simple fact that most executives, managers and employees don't know what their culture is, don't understand how corporate culture is formed, and don't understand the drivers that create corporate culture. Most managers have no clue as to whether their corporate culture is aligned with the business strategy, company values and supports effective execution, or whether it is a hindrance and out of alignment with company aims. It's this unknown factor that creates the biggest risk.

 Corporate culture shouldn't happen by accident, and if it does, there could be an accident.

Principle Four:
Culture Works on Human Logic, Not Business Logic

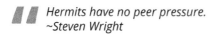 *Hermits have no peer pressure.*
~Steven Wright

Early humans had a pretty tough life as hunters and gatherers and to survive, belonging to a tribe and being accepted usually meant the difference between survival and death. Being accepted as a member of the tribe meant learning the skills and collective knowledge of the tribe and working together to hunt and fish in order to feed and clothe themselves and their families. Acceptance into the tribe, and thus a greater probability of survival, meant learning to do things that the group, and the leader, agreed with. Humans evolved as a social species and fitting into the group is hard-wired into our DNA and reinforced through social networks and peer pressure. In early times belonging to a group or tribe was necessary for survival. Today it often means keeping your job.

Because a business or organization is made up of people, it is no surprise to learn that peer pressure is a key driver and determinant of corporate culture. Today, a new employee who joins a company comes burdened with any number of pressing responsibilities, including a family, school fees and student loans, and usually a mortgage. It is critical for this new employee to fit in, to get along with his or her new teammates and boss, and to quickly learn how things are done in this new environment.

The innate human need to belong and be accepted as a member of a group is the same human process that drives social and fashion trends. In the 1960s there was no official declaration that acid-rock music, bell bottoms, long hair and tie-dyed t-shirts were required dress and behavior, yet within a few short months, young people the world over were dressed to fit in as part of a distinct tribe — Hippies — even if they didn't share the same beliefs. This tribe was a social and music trend that started with clothing and fashion, and ultimately became a political movement.

In 1996, the founders of Royal Elastics made a distinctive shoe that fastened with Velcro instead of laces. They believed their shoes looked cool and wanted to own the casual shoe market for trendy young adults. However, they had no marketing budget. Cleverly, they gave away free pairs of shoes to a number of underground DJs in London. DJs were trendsetters who young adults regarded as the vanguards of cool. Kids saw their idols, the DJs, wearing the shoes, and asked where they could get them. Within a year, the shoe became the biggest seller in Europe within their target market and in 2001 Royal Elastics was acquired by global shoe company K-Swiss.

Peer Pressure, Social Networks and Corporate Culture

When people are alone, their behavior tends to be a product of their upbringing, personal beliefs, attitudes, morals and habitual approaches to rules and regulations. They follow our own internal code of conduct and values. However, when people become part of a group, they subconsciously adopt the behavioral norms of the group even if those norms differ from their personal beliefs and behavior patterns. This shift in behavior is more likely to occur when one's pay check and future livelihood are at stake.

What Drives Employee Behavior (and Corporate Culture)?	
Alone	**In a Group or Organization**
• Personal values	• Pressure from leader of subgroup
• Goals or Desires	• Peer pressure
• Difficulty of action/task	• Desire to fit in
• Risk vs Reward	• Recognition
• Potential benefits	• Potential consequences
• Potential consequences	• Group norms
• Rules or laws	• Fear of being ostracized
• Hunger (physical state)	
• Fear (emotional state)	Copyright © 2017 John R Childress

An individual's behavior at work is determined more by peer pressure than official employer proclamations, the HR handbook, controls, rules or regulations. A closer look at much of the banking fraud and casino-like behavior inside of large banks reveals numerous sub-cultures, each of which have strong unwritten ground rules for how members should behave in order to *"fit in"* and remain a *"part of the group"*. And the huge bonuses on offer for those who *"make big money for the bank"* are an additional incentive to fit in and play the game. Thus peer pressure becomes a strong driver to adopt risky trading behaviors, or look the other way.

Experiments by psychologists in group behavior have consistently proven that even when individuals know what is right and know what should be done, many will not take the important step of speaking up or going against the collective group to which they belong.

Most people think of a corporate organization as a hierarchical social structure, with a boss at the top and various people with different skills and responsibilities cascading downward. In a hierarchical model, information and influence flow from top to bottom. Counter to traditional business thinking and logic, most organizations don't work in a top-down hierarchical fashion, but as a social network with a few key individuals acting as informal leaders and influencing how things are done much more than their position in the hierarchy would seem to suggest.

The following diagrams are of a typical company structure, showing the official organization chart (left), with Reilly leading the organization. The same organization, when mapped using an information technology approach called Organizational Network Analysis reveals that Cole, several levels down in the organization, has the largest number of social connections and exerts a strong influence on a great number of people and how things get done.[38] Culturally speaking, Cole is the informal trusted leader and the greatest influencer of the way work gets done in this company. Social network analysis of most companies shows that informal subcultures abound, centered on respected and trusted individuals like Cole.

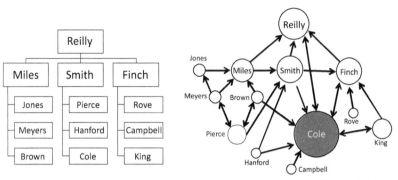

The human factor and social networks dominate organizations in every industry. At a hospital, the Head Nurse is usually a greater influencer of culture than the CEO, hospital administrator or senior doctors. In the military, the Master Sargent tends to be the key influencer of day-to-day behavior among the troops.

Informal leaders are cultural drivers who have a large influence on employee behavior inside a company. Corporate Values statements, risk guidelines, compliance regulations and even Codes of Conduct are weak culture drivers compared to the influence of informal leaders. Stories about highly respected and influential employees, even if they are long retired, are passed on to new employees and tend to drive the culture more than employee handbooks. At Home Depot, a *"care for the customer"* culture has been immortalized in the story of an employee telling a customer that he didn't need to buy a new $200 faucet because the faucet could be fixed with a $1.50 part. For the CEO and leadership team that understands this principle of peer pressure, the concept can be used to drive significant culture change, and performance improvement.

Peer Pressure and a Business Turnaround

By the middle of the 1990s, Continental Airlines was on the verge of bankruptcy. In the eyes of both business and holiday customers it was a lousy airline to fly. Flights were often late taking off and landing, baggage was either lost or damaged, and business customers routinely missed connecting flights and important business meetings.

With an understanding of the principle that culture works on human logic not business logic, CEO Gordon Bethune and the senior team came up with a simple *"Go Forward"* plan for using peer pressure to turn the company's culture around. Under the new plan, every employee in the company — from the cleaners to the CEO — was to be given a $65 bonus every month the company ranked in the top 5 of the airline industry statistics for on-time performance. With this policy, Continental steadily rose in Department of Transportation airline statistics in on-time performance, as well as fewest lost luggage incidents and fewest customer complaints until it was leading the league tables, and becoming a highly profitable airline.

Bethune's *"Go Forward"* plan recognized that there's an aspect to incentives which is not necessarily about money. In this case, while $65 is not a huge individual incentive, not working hard or efficiently would not just cause you to lose your own $65 bonus, but also negatively impact everyone else's bonus. Incentives in a linked system tend to be driven by peer pressure and the human need to fit in with the group. No one wanted to be known as the person, or department, that let the entire company down.[39]

Peer pressure is the most powerful driver and shaper of corporate culture, and peer pressure within an organization is strongly correlated with business performance and how we do things around here. Few leaders understand how to use this principle effectively. As with the Continental example, positive incentives, combined with positive peer pressure and good leadership can create exceptional performance.

 Gentlemen! We must, indeed, all hang together or, most assuredly, we shall all hang separately.
~Benjamin Franklin

Principle Five:

Organizations are Shadows of their Leaders

> *What you are thunders so loud that*
> *I cannot hear what you say. ~Ralph Waldo Emerson*

Shortly after Alan Mulally became CEO of Ford Motor Company in 2006, he realized the fate of the company rested on restoring liquidity, making some hard operational choices about costs and brands, and changing the culture. To reshape the cost-driven, silo-focused culture to a *"One Ford"* culture focused on shared objectives, speed and accountability, Mulally began using a very different leadership style than his predecessors. Convinced that excessive and lengthy emails were a clear sign of an impersonal, risk averse and slow-to-respond culture, he responded to emails in person or by telephone, even if the message came from lower level employees. Stories began to circulate about the new boss and his open communication style and his sincere interest in listening to ideas.

Mulally's behavior was different from the traditional formal, hierarchical and aloof behavior that was common at Ford. Through individual acts of reaching out and connecting with people, he built up the morale of a tired, failing and insecure organization. Alan Mulally became Cheerleader in Chief, and people responded to his optimistic and direct style.

> *The most powerful leadership tool you have is your own*
> *personal example. ~John Wooden, legendary basketball coach*

Then he went even further to establish a more open, transparent culture. He set up a weekly 4-hour videoconference meeting with all Ford senior executives around the world and invited each leader to share their wins and problems and to highlight their weekly business results. Mulally never chastised anyone for poor results, but instead kept asking the same question: *"What do you need from us to get on track?"*.

The new CEO continued his culture change campaign through hiring when he recruited his new CFO from Ford of Europe, Lewis Booth, to model the same behaviors within the strong and powerful Ford finance function. For decades the finance function in Ford had enormous power over how things were done, focusing heavily on repeated cost reductions, and even putting people on the spot for not knowing all the financial details of their business. Internal finance policies and processes were strong drivers of the old Ford culture.

The old Ford culture of never admitting to problems for fear of public humiliation kept people from asking for help or admitting to problems early on. When executives needed support from other areas of expertise within Ford, they questioned whether they could trust the other functions and regions to support them. Low trust resulted in slow speed of decision making and higher operating costs.

Over several months, a consistent pattern of new behavior by Mulally and Booth built enough trust throughout Ford that before long, problems and solutions were flying around the Ford global empire. The old silo culture had been broken by consistent and congruent leadership behaviors. Ford now had a recovery plan, growing cross-functional teamwork, and leadership they could believe in. To maintain the new culture, the senior team carried pocket cards with the Ford recovery plan and the new expected leadership behaviors, which they would often pull out and use in meetings and when coaching staff and others.

Go Further

ONE FORD

ONE TEAM · ONE PLAN · ONE GOAL

ONE TEAM
People working together as a lean, global enterprise to make people's lives better through automotive and mobility leadership, as measured by:
Customer, Employee, Dealer, Investor, Supplier, Union/Council, and Community Satisfaction

ONE PLAN
- Aggressively restructure to operate profitably at the current demand and changing model mix
- Accelerate development of new products, services and experiences customers want and value
- Finance our plan and maintain a strong balance sheet
- Work together effectively as one team

ONE GOAL
An exciting viable Ford delivering profitable growth for all

Foster Functional and Technical Excellence · Know and have a passion for our business and our customers · Demonstrate and build functional and technical excellence · Ensure process discipline · Have a continuous improvement philosophy and practice

Own Working Together · Believe in skilled and motivated people working together · Include everyone; respect, listen to, help and appreciate others · Build strong relationships; be a team player; develop ourselves and others · Communicate clearly, concisely and candidly

Role Model Ford Values · Move fast with an innovation mindset in everything we do · Show initiative, courage, integrity and good corporate citizenship · Improve quality, safety and sustainability · Have a can do, find a way attitude and emotional resilience · Enjoy the journey and each other; have fun – never at others' expense

Deliver Results · Deal positively with our business realities; develop compelling and comprehensive plans, while keeping an enterprise view · Set high expectations and inspire others · Make sound decisions using facts and data · Hold ourselves and others responsible and accountable for delivering results and satisfying our customers

www.one.ford.com

People buy into the leader before they buy into the vision.
~John C. Maxwell

A leader's actions and behaviors cast a powerful shadow across an organization. It is important to remember that actions speak louder than words. People watch the behavior of their leaders for clues as to what is accepted and what is not. When a leader says one thing and then behaves differently, employees quickly figure out the real story. The longest shadows are cast during times of crisis. These moments of truth are perpetuated in stories passed from employee to employ. Stories about how leaders behave in crisis have a significant impact on defining a company's culture.

Organizations are shadows of their leaders.
That's the good news and the bad news.

Drew Houston, CEO and co-founder of Dropbox, became so annoyed with staff showing up late for work and meetings that he called an all-hands meeting to talk about timeliness. However, Drew showed up late, blaming the taxi and bad traffic, and then launched into his demands for timeliness. At the end of the meeting a young engineer asked to speak with Houston in private. He told the CEO that the behavior of tardiness was bigger than just heavy traffic, which everyone has experienced. Actually what people were feeling about the CEO and the company was a perceived lack of respect for staff and was interpreted as rules don't apply to the CEO. His words struck a powerful chord with Houston about the impact of leadership behavior on culture.

> *We can write down all the pretty words about our culture and values that we want. But people will pay a thousand times more attention to what you do as a leader than what you say. It's all the little things leaders do, that they might not even realize, that set the standards for the team.* [40]

The shadow effect of leaders and leadership teams is measurable. Many years ago, I developed a proprietary **Culture Assessment Questionnaire** to provide leadership teams with a visual understanding of the best and worst aspects of their current culture, as well as the impact they have as a team on the entire organization.

The chart below is an example of a culture profile from an organization that obviously needs to improve its performance in several areas, but also has some real strengths. What you see below is how the senior team sees itself and the company's culture with respect to several important business categories, color-coded to draw attention to both positives and negatives. The three colored bands, red, yellow and green correspond to the stoplight system of danger, caution and go.

As you can see, the senior team rates itself high to average in some areas and low in others. This survey is usually used to spark some lengthy, and sometimes emotional, discussions in our leadership and culture workshop sessions. And in this particular company formed the foundation for several strategic initiatives to improve performance and competitiveness.

What is even more insightful for a senior team is how the next level, their direct reports, view the culture! Here is the same survey given to the direct reports of the senior team, and plotted along with the Sr. Team responses.

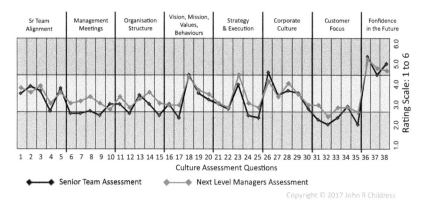

Nearly a perfect mirror image! And in all my 35+ years of working with senior leadership teams, these two assessments almost always mirror each other. And the next level of leaders in turn influence a large population of employees. Organizations are shadows of their leaders.

As leaders change their individual and collective behaviors, the behavior and performance of a company also begins to shift. Below is a chart from a company that in 2003 was facing bankruptcy after releasing a defective product resulting in several customer deaths. As you can see, the senior team was demoralized and thought poorly of the company culture. With new leadership and a focus on building new organizational capabilities and a sense of pride in the company and its products, the scores on the same culture assessment rose dramatically, as did the company's performance. This same company is now back into a position of market leadership and recently won the distinguished North American Shingo Prize for Manufacturing Excellence.

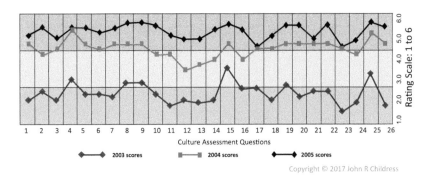

Culture Assessment Questions

◆——◆ 2003 scores   ■——■ 2004 scores   ◆——◆ 2005 scores

The behavior of senior executives can set and reinforce company culture on a daily basis. In a study by Bain & Co., assessing data from 1990 to 2014, it was found that founder-led companies performed 3.1 times better than non-founder led S&P 500 companies.[41] Founders who are still in place cast a powerful shadow far down into the organization because they tend to be more zealous about the culture and employee behavior than externally recruited leaders. This superior performance can be attributed to the *"founder mentality"*, which consists of the following key traits:

- o A sense of insurgent mission
- o An obsession with the front line
- o An owner's mindset and a deep feeling of personal responsibility

Founders still active in the business are more willing to intervene when they see behavior counter to the required culture. They have the courage and conviction to step in at coachable moments and actively redirect attitudes and behaviors, instead of walking on by. Founders cast exceptionally strong shadows.

Fading Shadows

The influence of leaders and the senior team on corporate culture is not uniform across time. In start-ups and early stage companies, the senior team, including the founder(s), tend to set the ground rules for culture. The recent trend towards the production of Culture Decks and the development of strong on-boarding programs to stress culture is one way leaders cast a strong shadow. In small to medium sized organizations where employees have frequent contact with senior executives, the behavior of the leaders has great influence in establishing the culture and the ways of working.

Things are different in large and well-established companies. Here, the impact of leadership behaviors fades dramatically, replaced by the significant influence of peer pressure and fueled by the very real human need of employees to fit in with their workgroup and not be seen as an outsider. The chart below describes the falling and rising influence of these two culture drivers on establishing and sustaining corporate culture.

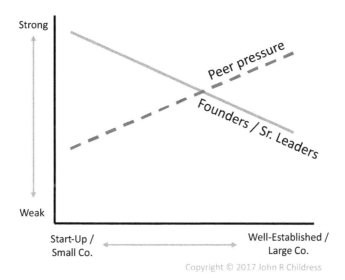

In many discussions of corporate culture, the impact of the leader (CEO), and leadership team has been over-exaggerated. As a result, many of us looking to understand corporate culture, how it is formed and how it is sustained, have overlooked the powerful cultural lever of peer group pressure.

The Dark Side of Leadership Shadows

There is also a dark side to the impact of leadership behavior on the organization. Several recent research studies are beginning to show causal linkages between poor leadership, toxic management behaviors and employee distress and illness.

 A bad leader can ruin a good culture faster than a good leader can turnaround a bad culture.

More than thirty studies have clearly shown that the behavior of leaders affect employee health.[42] The overall research shows that positive leader behaviors can reduce sick leave, increase attendance and reduce anxiety, depression, stress and burnout. Negative behaviors, on the other hand, including excessive micromanagement, public humiliation, demanding long hours, constantly raising expectations and goals, and other stressful behaviors from leaders and bosses can increase heart disease, promote musculoskeletal pain, foster sick leave, increase anxiety and depression, as well as lead to burnout.

On the whole, these studies clearly imply that bad bosses have a multiplier effect far down into the organization. As a result, a whole new field of litigation is opening – lawsuits against toxic managers and the organizations that negligently allow them to supervise employees. If corporate culture is influenced and sustained by the repetitive and habitual behaviors of its leadership and employees, then it won't be long before toxic or dysfunctional corporate cultures will be cited in more and more employee health lawsuits, just as it has been citied in lawsuits about industrial accidents and poor safety practices.

In fact, this trend has already begun. Brokerage firm Merrill Lynch settled a lawsuit for $160 million that claimed the company culture was toxic for African Americans.[43] Likewise, Fox News Corporation is the subject of multiple ongoing workplace lawsuits claiming that the company tolerates harassment, discrimination and retaliation. In short, the lawsuits attack Fox News' workplace culture.

 Organizations are shadows of their leaders ...
that's the good news and the bad news!

Principle Six:
Cultural Drift

 Every day you spend drifting away from your goals is a waste not only of that day, but also of the additional day it takes to regain lost ground. ~ Ralph Marston

There is now conclusive evidence that the continents on our planet have been slowly moving as a result of subsea volcanic activity in a process called plate tectonics and continental drift. From one solid landmass about 300 million years ago, which paleontologists named Pangaea, the continents broke away and slowly moved to their current positions. And they are still moving today, albeit at the rate of only about 1 inch per year.

The analogy between continental drift and shifts over time in corporate culture is quite clear and forms one of the important culture principles that helps improve business performance.

Almost all early stage companies have some sort of foundational principles, usually based on the beliefs and values of the founders, about how to build a successful business, how to treat employees and how to develop work processes. Only a few companies carefully codify their start-up cultures, although to do so is becoming more common. Netflix developed its Culture Deck, a 124-slide presentation on the Netflix culture, values and behaviors. HubSpot, Amazon, Google and Zappos. com also have rigorous new employee on-boarding processes which help establish accepted ways of working inside the company, and prove highly useful in establishing alignment between employees and organizational objectives.

 The problem with most organizations as they grow and change is that nearly everything gets managed, often micro-managed, except the culture.

Culture is often left to evolve on its own, and as a result organizations experience cultural drift. As the culture shifts, employee behavior can easily get out of alignment with the organization's strategic objectives and mission. Much of this drift is the result of an influx of new employees who come from companies with different cultures and ways of working. The establishment of company operations in other regions and countries can also contribute to the drift and fragmentation of the original culture.

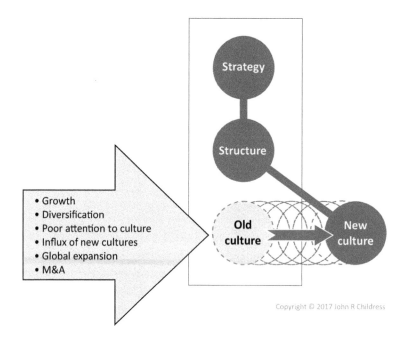

One of the prime reasons so many well-aligned cultures shift out of alignment over time is that executives at the top rarely understand or appreciate the importance of corporate culture on performance.

With practices in more than 30 countries, the Arthur Andersen accounting firm was once the envy of the professional services world, with a strong reputation for integrity and for being the best place to work. The early founders and senior leaders of the firm actively managed the culture by requiring all employees to attend the Andersen training center in St. Charles, Illinois. By 1991 over 50,000 employees annually were trained and indoctrinated into their unique corporate culture. Much of this training focused on the *"Andersen Way"*, which contained proprietary methodologies for auditing and consulting, as well as a large dose of culture and values. It was the prize company to work for among the major global accounting firms and they recruited the best and brightest from business schools. Andersen employees happily referred to themselves as *"Androids"*.

In 2002, indictments during the Enron investigation forced Arthur Andersen into bankruptcy. Most outsiders believed the greed and fraud by Enron officers combined with illegalities of a few Andersen auditors was the cause.

 Arthur Andersen, once the world's most admired auditing and professional services firm, descended through level after level of self-destructive decline to its ultimate death.
~Charles Ellis

Although the Enron scandal was the last straw, Andersen's demise stemmed from a cultural drift that had begun decades before.

Charles Ellis, in his book, *What it Takes: Seven secrets of success from the world's greatest professional firms,*[44] traces the firm's decline to the time when its leaders shifted their focus from the cornerstones of the Andersen culture and business reputation (client service, professional integrity and quality) to competing against the other global accounting and consulting firms for growth in revenues and market position. The company's goal shifted from being the best to being the biggest.

In its quest to be the biggest, Andersen expanded around the world and abandoned practices geared toward professional excellence, such as their long established rule that all accountants must spend two years in auditing. They also abandoned their unique global profit pool that ensured all partners had a stake in one another's success. Each change in the internal work policies and practices, while defensible to support the new vision, pushed the firm further and further away from its original values and culture.

Cultural drift also made it easier to ignore an increasing number of warning signs, including the 1973 bankruptcy of Four Seasons Nursing Centers of America, in which the founder pleaded guilty to securities fraud and Andersen, as the auditor, was indicted. By the time Enron became a key client in the late 1990s, the firm's once highly professional culture had drifted past the point of no return.

Fragmentation and Subcultures

A culture can easily drift from its original values and work practices as a result of neglect or lazy leadership. Given the strong pressures inherent in global expansion, mergers and acquisitions, hiring from the outside and frequent leadership changes, it is easy to see how multiple subcultures can evolve as a means for employees to find a group to identify with and belong.

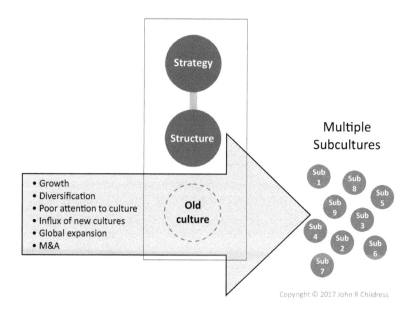

In one sense, subcultures are a natural part of any organization. Subcultures can be defined as *"groups of organizational members who interact regularly with each other, identify themselves as a distinct group within that organization, share the same problems, and take action on the basis of a common way of thinking that is unique to the group"*. [45]

If leadership ignores the management of corporate culture, the need for belonging to a group interested in more than quarterly profits draws employees to form tightly-knit subcultures. Usually led by an employee that the group trusts and respects, the human need for belonging and being accepted into a group makes these subcultures remarkably strong. When they are aligned with the overall company strategy and ways of working, subcultures provide a direct connection between company strategy and daily work activities. When subcultures form that are out of alignment with the overall values and business strategies, they can be a considerable barrier to strategy execution and a major blockage to change initiatives.

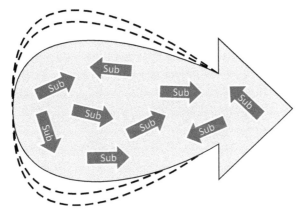

Subcultures out of alignment with overall strategy.
Internal tension, Poor execution

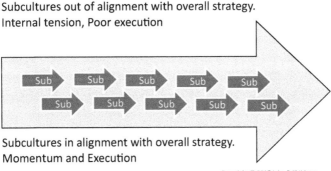

Subcultures in alignment with overall strategy.
Momentum and Execution

No company can escape the forces of change. To ignore these forces and, in doing so, to hold on to outdated products or services, or to ignore the changing expectations of today's workforce, is a design for failure. Yet a culture that has been designed from the beginning around the customer and that evolves as customer needs shift should be protected, for it is the foundation for future success.

Jeff Bezos, CEO of Amazon, has a unique view on strategic, commercial change. Bezos designed the Amazon business model and corporate culture around delivering customer value, and he believes this mission to be the one thing that will not change at Amazon in the years to come:

 I very frequently get the question: "What's going to change in the next 10 years?" I almost never get the question: "What's not going to change in the next 10 years?" And I submit to you that that second question is actually the more important of the two — because you can build a business strategy around the things that are stable in time. In our retail business, we know that customers want low prices, and I know that's going to be true 10 years from now. It's impossible to imagine a future where a customer comes up and says, "Jeff I love Amazon; I just wish the prices were a little higher", [or] "I love Amazon; I just wish you'd deliver a little more slowly".

Principle Seven:
Policies Drive Culture (More Than We Realize)

 First we shape our institutions; thereafter they shape us.
~Winston Churchill

When most observers search for evidence of corporate culture, what they easily find are the visible, habitual behaviors associated with how employees get things done. These behaviors are not the culture itself, but merely the visible outcomes of the corporate culture system. Business policies, work processes and internal practices are among the strongest drivers of corporate culture.

There is little doubt that recruitment and selection, socialization, training and development, performance management, and compensation and benefits contribute directly to an organization's ability to attract and retain good employees... these practices contribute indirectly to an organization's ability to retain its best employees through their impact on organizational culture.[46]

The illegal and fraudulent activities within the global banking industry played a large role in the global economic meltdown that began in 2008. What drove such excess behavior and activities in a profession once considered the paragon of ethics and professionalism? After all, bankers have the fiduciary and moral responsibility of looking after other people's money and for decades did so with integrity and concerned stewardship.

Change the Policies, Change the Behaviors

Two significant changes in the financial services industry brought about a massive change in the internal working practices and behaviors of those in global banking. First came the 1999 repeal of Glass-Steagall Act, which for decades separated retail from investment banking. Traditionally, retail bankers were the paragons of integrity and ethics, while the privately held investment banks made their money through the riskier areas of trading, financing, investing and advisory services. The repeal of Glass-Steagall allowed the investment firms and the investment divisions of large global banks access to a larger pool of capital for increasingly risky investments for the purpose of growing brank profits and shareholder value. Additionally, senior investment bankers were hired to be the CEO at most of the major retail banking institutions. At the same time interest rates moved to an all-time low such that a large amount of low-interest money became available for home buyers and investors, which banks and financial advisory firms aggressively promoted. There were huge profits to be made and the banks were first in line.

In order to capitalize on this rare economic and regulatory environment, banks began to beef up their advisory, investment and trading organizations by shifting the traditional bank hiring profile from conservative, accounting and finance majors to smart, aggressive and ambitious young men and women with a penchant for sales. The brightest and most aggressive flooded into the major banks and were tutored in how to sell financial instruments that would earn large returns for the bank. Customer welfare took a distant second place to the bank generating greater profits. To keep these bright, aggressive and status-driven new recruits, internal bank compensation policies shifted towards larger and larger bonuses and performance incentives. In the words of one senior banker, it was a *"perfect storm"* as easy money met loose morals and greed.

 The motto of the old order in the City of London was, 'My word is my bond', but the financial crisis revealed a culture quite alien to that heritage. The stewards of people's money were revealed to have been speculators with it. ~Gordon Brown

While this is an extreme situation, there is no denying that internal compensation policies drive behavior. The compensation drivers behind teamwork and individualism are very different. Customer focus and personal gain are driven by different compensation policies and performance bonus systems. A firm's compensation system also acts as a filter in recruiting, either attracting or deterring certain personality types.[47]

Another important culture driver is the company budgeting process. In many companies, budgets that are established early in the fiscal year drive how managers behave in terms of investments in people, capital equipment and training. In most companies, if an item was not included in the original budget, chances are it won't get funded. Consequently, a falloff in revenue and rising costs of materials often results in headcount reductions in order to keep the budget in line. Downsizing and offshoring are activities often driven by attempts to keep the original budget and margins in line. A company driven by strict budgets often develops a culture of risk aversion and weak innovation.

Stock options for employees have been positively linked to cultures with higher productivity, innovation and engagement. Ascend Communications is a technology and telecoms start-up that grew rapidly from its founding in 1988, and reinvented itself three times to take advantage of shifts in digital technology and telecoms regulation. In 1999 Lucent Technologies merged with Ascend Communications for $20 billion, the largest such deal in the history of the data networking industry.

Rob Ryan, co-founder and CEO of Ascend, believes that providing stock options for all employees was a major driver of the Ascend culture, known for change agility, innovation and employees behaving like owners. Currently Ryan is a private investor in start-ups and an advisor to many emerging growth companies and will only invest in a company with employee stock ownership as a part of the culture.

Meetings, Meetings, Meetings

The structure, processes and frequency of meetings inside a company also has a significant impact on corporate culture. In many ways, meetings are a microcosm of a company culture, yet those who call and run meetings rarely consider them as culture drivers and how they impact overall business performance.[48] In numerous ways, bad meetings send negative messages to employees about the quality of the company and its leadership.

If you had to identify, in one word, the reason why the human race has not achieved, and never will achieve, its full potential, that word would be "meetings".
~Dave Barry

In a world where everything is moving faster and faster, speed of decision making and execution are the new currency. Yet most companies have not re-designed their meetings for greater effectiveness. In fact, most internal company meetings are so inefficient and a waste of time that many attendees focus on email and other tasks during meetings instead of actively participating.

Intel, known for innovation and execution, has developed a mandatory internal training course on meeting effectiveness as part of the required on-boarding process. The course was designed by legendary Intel CEO Andy Grove himself as a way to build and maintain a corporate culture of innovation and speeds as a competitive advantage.

Culture and Workplace Design

When modern corporations began to take shape in the early 20th Century, office design closely mirrored the military organization charts of the time, with senior offices at the top of the building with corner offices, managers getting internal offices and employees in large open spaces containing rows of identical desks. Those with offices closest to the senior leaders were regarded as having more power within the company. The business world has changed radically as a result of information availability and the demands for cross-functional collaboration. Yet most companies continue to use space without understanding its impact on culture and productivity.

Few companies understand the impact of office space and design on corporate culture and people productivity better than Steelcase, the global office design and furniture company with approximately 11,000 employees and $3.1 billion in revenue. Former CEO James Hackett turned around Steelcase by understanding that people and productivity are at the heart of company performance, and use of space can enhance or block creativity and information sharing.

 Innovation requires collective 'we' work. To this end, it's critical to design spaces that not only support collaboration, but augment it (with) spaces that promote eye-to-eye contact,

*provide everyone with equal access to information, and allow
people to move around and participate freely. ~James Hackett*

Pixar has a huge open atrium engineering environment where staff run into each other throughout the day and interact in informal, unplanned ways. While mayor of New York City, Michael Bloomberg preferred his staff sit in a "bullpen" environment instead of separate offices with soundproof doors. Technology firms cluster in Silicon Valley and many adopt the open-plan architecture typical to start-ups. Financial firms cluster in London and New York. Place and space shapes culture.

When you want a culture of collaboration across functions, you can use office layout to help build such a culture. For example, one CEO described how they used the placement of the coffee machine as a culture driver.

 Our office in Switzerland has three floors with a little cafe on the ground level that has a nice coffee machine. We could have put a coffee machine on each floor in that building. But the flow in that building would be completely different than it is today, where if you want to have a coffee you have to walk down the stairs, go to the cafe, make a coffee. Most of the time you'll see 10 or 12 people in that cafe, and they might be from different businesses, or one person might be in supply chain, another person might be in product management. Imagine the interfaces that occur just for that reason that otherwise might not.[49]

National cultures impact office design and layout because attitudes toward personal space differ greatly from country to country. Germans prefer more solitude and German companies allocate an average of 320 square feet per employee, while in America the average is 190. In India and China, personal space allocations are 70 and 50 square feet respectively.

Culture and HR Policies

The most ubiquitous corporate culture drivers are the HR systems and policies. The Human Resource function has multiple culture levers at its disposal, yet few HR leaders critically assess the impact of HR policies and practices on culture and what work behaviors and attitudes these policies promote.

Strong culture drivers are contained in pay systems, performance evaluations, on-boarding, promotion criteria, employee recognition schemes, recruiting and hiring profiles, medical and health policies, training and professional development. To effectively impact corporate culture, HR systems should drive not only job performance, but also behaviors. Savvy companies have learned to use these powerful culture drivers as incentives for recruiting, engagement and employee retention.

John Brandon, a Vice President of Sales for Apple created a pocket card that was given to new employees during orientation, with 11 tips for success.[50] And he role-modelled the eleven principles as well.

1. Let go of the old, make the most of the future.
2. Always tell the truth, we want to hear the bad news sooner than later
3. The highest level of integrity is expected, when in doubt, ask
4. Learn to be a good businessperson, not just a good salesperson
5. Everyone sweeps the floor
6. Be professional in your style, speech and follow-up
7. Listen to the customer, they almost always get it right
8. Create win/win relationships with our partners
9. Look out for each other, sharing information is a good thing
10. Don't take yourself too seriously
11. Have fun, otherwise it's not worth it

Tip number 5, *"Everyone sweeps the floor"*, is particularly powerful in helping build and sustain the Apple culture. One Apple employee explained it as:

 It means that no job is too 'low level' or unimportant for anyone to help with. In other words, don't get a big head just because you work for Apple or you got a promotion or you're making $X per year — the basics still matter, and you'll always be expected to help regardless of how high up you rise or how fancy you think you are.[50]

If competitive advantage is dependent upon cross-functional teamwork and collaboration, HR can establish team-based recognition and reward programs. They can also develop performance management processes that let peers as well as supervisors evaluate teamwork and collaboration. Training programs can be designed to foster open communications, collaboration and trust, while recruiting policies can focus on those individuals who have demonstrated an ability to work well in teams and experience in leading cross-functional teams. And supervisor and management training can help develop skills for the effective leadership and management of a team-based culture.

Company policies and work practices have a profound impact on employee behavior, yet very few work policies are designed with behaviors in mind. In fact, most policies are established without any thought as to how they shape the corporate culture. This is analogous to the situation where the product design function develops new products and then sends the drawings and specifications to manufacturing, only to find that due to material constraints and tolerances, the products have flaws built into the designs. Excessive waste, rework, warranty costs and product liability claims were the natural result.

A more effective approach, called design-for-manufacturability, pairs up designers with manufacturing engineers during the entire development process, ensuring that product build, performance and costs are all in line. We believe company work policies and practices should be designed with the business strategy and culture requirements in mind in order to create greater internal alignment between strategy, structure and culture.

The interesting thing about all these strong drivers of corporate culture is they are not difficult to change, if senior management understands the value and impact of culture and has the courage to reshape internal policies. Many companies have policies that seem to be sacrosanct, and changing them is considered off limits. Senior leaders are often reluctant to shift, revise, or even review legacy company policies which were in place before they arrived. Turnaround specialists are beginning to see the value of designing behavioral outcomes into their turnaround business models and rethinking work policies which will drive a culture of accountability, teamwork, execution, customer focus and innovation.

 Here is my first principle of foreign policy:
good government at home. ~William E. Gladstone

Principle Eight:

You Get the Culture You Ignore

Most corporate disasters are crimes of ambivalence, not crimes of passion.

The following scenario happens repeatedly inside every company. A small group of employees are standing around the coffee machine as one upset employee shares her frustration about another department. *"You just can't rely on them for anything! They obviously have their own agenda and any request for information and help goes into a black hole and never comes out. They really don't care about the customer, just their own budgets and department goals. Yet whenever they need some information, they demand it right away and are very unpleasant. I've had it with them and the next time they need my help they are going to get some of their own medicine!"* The small crowd nods their heads in agreement and several add additional examples of how uncooperative that department is and definitely not team players.

This idle talk may seem harmless, but attitudes about others in the workplace impact how we behave towards them. In a company where cross-functional collaboration is a competitive advantage, such beliefs and attitudes about other departments or individuals can easily lead to resistance of requests for information, slow turnaround times, working to rule and other dysfunctional behaviors.

Leaders get the culture they deserve.
~Seth Godin

But here's what makes these seemingly benign human interactions and bad-mouthing even worse. Imagine that during this venting around the coffee machine a senior manager or VP casually walks buy and overhears the negative conversations.

So what happens next? Well, in 90% of the cases the VP continues walking. After all, it's not their department, and they're already late for a meeting. The VP makes a mental note to talk to the VP in charge of that department, but by the end of the busy day it is forgotten.

Hundreds of coachable moments happen every day inside companies, but most land on the pile of missed opportunities as leaders choose not to get involved. The rationale may be acceptable, but the leadership behavior is not. When leaders choose not to get involved and avoid intervening and redirecting these types of conversations, they are actually condoning attitudes and beliefs counter to the culture they say they want in the company.

Culture, Courage and "Coachable Moments"

Since culture reveals itself as habitual behaviors, if managers don't intervene and coach peers and employees when they see inappropriate behavior, these quickly become the norm; the way we do things around here. Every workday is filled with *"coachable moments"* to help build and sustain a strong and aligned culture. Most are missed due to lack of leadership courage.

When leaders fail to challenge negative attitudes and behavior in meetings, it's a signal to all that such behavior is condoned. When co-workers fail to challenge each other concerning poor attitudes or behavior, the negativity is seen as normal, tends to spread and in many cases escalates into lack of trust and reduced employee engagement.

There's an old African proverb that says it takes a village to raise a child. In modern organizations it takes everyone to build and maintain the corporate culture. Corporate culture is not a top-down invention, and it can't be maintained or reshaped by leaders alone. Every employee is accountable for the type of workplace culture they want.

Our privileges can be no greater than our obligations. The protection of our rights can endure no longer than the performance of our responsibilities. ~John F. Kennedy

Most leaders and managers will intervene when they come across cases of truly bad behavior, but often hesitate when it comes to conversations or behaviors that aren't overly negative, but definitely don't fit the desired culture. When this happens, the opportunity to take advantage of a coachable moment is lost. The executive may grumble about such poor attitudes, usually to their peers, but rarely will they take a stand, talk to the individual or group, explain that such behavior or attitudes are not useful or helpful in this company and ask why they are behaving that way. More often than not, such firm and direct dialogue uncovers some level of personal or workplace-related frustration, which may include a real issue that needs attention.

Another interesting aspect of stepping in at coachable moments is the impact it has on people observing the encounter. For example, when an executive in a meeting misses their promised delivery date or goal, how the meeting leader behaves at that coachable moment will send a signal not only to that one executive, but to everyone around the table. Letting it go or harshly reprimanding the person casts a long shadow, as does using the event as a positive coachable moment to reinforce the responsibilities of leadership.

Complaining about attitudes and behavior is not leadership, but taking a stand on behalf of the few non-negotiable behaviors that define the company culture is. Most executives fail the test, and under their supervision the company's culture drifts more and more towards unproductive employee behaviors.

The 2013 Deloitte Core Beliefs & Culture survey of over 1000 employees and 300 executives reported that 81% of executives and 86% of employees believe that declared cultural behaviors are not upheld inside their organizations.[51] The obvious conclusion from this data is that a significant number of behaviors and actions not in alignment with the desired culture are being consistently ignored or tolerated.

 You get the culture you tolerate!
You reinforce the behaviors you ignore.

How many *'coachable moments'* have you walked right by? Does your management team understand it is their job to engage and redirect behaviors? Do employees feel empowered to step up and step in!

You build the culture you want through engaging in coachable moments. And building and sustaining a culture is everyone's job!

 If you are building a culture where honest expectations are communicated and peer accountability is the norm, then the group will address poor performance and attitudes.
~Henry Cloud

Principle Nine:

There Is No Perfect Corporate Culture

 Perfection is not attainable, but if we chase perfection we can catch excellence. ~Vince Lombardi

---

No two corporate cultures are the same, and yet some cultures are more effective at supporting and driving execution and results than others. Trying to design or shape the perfect corporate culture is impossible, but there are several cultural elements that if well designed and supported, can lead to culture being a significant competitive advantage.

 At its best, an organization's culture is an immense source of value. It enables, energizes, and enhances its employees and thus fosters ongoing high performance. At its worst, the culture can be a drag on productivity and emotional commitment, undermining long-term success. Most companies are so large and complex that the culture acts in both ways at once. Indeed, the culture of a large company is typically made up of several interwoven subcultures, all affecting and responding to one another. ~Jon Katzenbach [52]

Align Culture and Strategy

Probably the most important requirement for culture as a competitive advantage is alignment between the culture and the business strategy.

Strategy defines a winning value proposition, which requires not only a matching business model, but specific employee behaviors in order to deliver sustainable value to customers.

To create alignment between strategy and corporate culture, it is important for senior management to first define the specific work behaviors that would best support the delivery of the business strategy. For example, Alan Mulally needed to reshape the Ford culture to drive the turnaround strategy he and the senior team had developed. One of the challenges was a legacy culture of *"no bad news"* and *"shoot the messenger"*, as well as mistrust and lack of openness between functions and departments. These ingrained habitual attitudes and behaviors were the opposite of what was required for his goal of creating a One Ford culture and a return to profitability.

In order to align culture and strategy, the Ford senior team developed a series of Breakthrough Objectives that combined business and culture issues into a single document that was easy for every employee to understand the relevance of these breakthroughs to their individual jobs. Each element of the Ford Breakthrough Objectives had a number of examples and stories developed that described specifically how the new behaviors were translated into everyday work life. These stories became the core content of every presentation management made to employees, customers and the press. Mulally was a master at telling the One Ford story using examples from all the global regions where Ford manufactured and sold vehicles.

Ford Breakthrough Objectives

PEOPLE
Working Together Globally
- "Tell the Truth"
- One Ford Culture
- Superior Sales and Service

PRODUCT
Best-in-Class Vehicles
- Focus on the Blue Oval
- Lead in Quality, Safety, Fuel Efficiency
- Build cars people want to buy

MARKETPLACE
Global Responsibility
- Operate "Globally"
- Take a positive stand for the environment
- Match capacity with business

FINANCIAL
Fund the Future
- Secure Liquidity
- Grow the business profitably

In a recent series of articles and webinars on culture and strategy by Jon Katzenbach and Paul Leinwand, partners in the PwC organization, Strategy&, the authors put forth the proposition that the right strategic choice for a company out of several options is the one that best fits your current culture.[53] Trying to implement a new strategy while at the same time reshaping corporate culture is a monumental task, and it is rarely successful. Working within the current culture and reshaping a few key behaviors is the best way to embed a new strategy and deliver on strategic objectives.

 Culture is the oil that makes the company's value creation engine turn frictionless ~Jon Katzenbach

As business academics John Kotter, Clayton Christensen and Jim Collins suggest, cultures which are flexible and adaptable, with a high degree of innovation and tolerance for risk are better suited for today's global, fast moving and highly competitive business landscape. Whatever specific behaviors are required to align culture and strategy, there are some elements of culture that almost all companies with long track records of success tend to possess. Those common culture drivers are open communications in all directions, trust and respect up and down, innovation and the encouragement of new ideas, and perhaps most importantly, a single minded focus on customer needs and creating sustainable customer value.

Culture as Brand

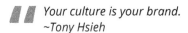 *Your culture is your brand.*
~Tony Hsieh

While there is no perfect corporate culture, having a distinctive culture that aligns the brand image, employee experience and customer experience is one of the best ways for culture to power business success, competitive advantage and employee engagement.

Much time and money is often spent by companies to develop their brand image. Numerous large PR agencies specialize in helping organizations with brand development, brand messaging and even logo design. Logos are crafted to reflect the brand. Multichannel ads are developed. A current trend is short, catchy video stories using stunning visuals and evocative settings to convey the desired brand characteristics. Volvo uses a series of short, inviting video ads featuring its Swedish heritage.[54] Coca-Cola has been the master of branding and video ads for decades, displaying its brand values of refreshment and enjoying life with friends. In every industry brand imaging is being used to position the positive characteristics of the company and its products in the minds of customer. Brand is also used to distinguish and distance a company from its competitors.

 Your brand is a promise to your customers.
Your corporate culture is a promise to your employees.

But when brand and culture are out of alignment, the customer notices! Customers rebel, employees get turned off, and company performance suffers. One telltale sign of this lack of alignment is whether employees are treated differently than customers. You can't expect employees to deliver benefits to customers that they don't experience themselves. If the brand image and brand values are not built into the employee experience, from hiring, to on-boarding, to performance reviews, to product development processes, to rewards and recognition, it will be difficult for these same employees to deliver on the brand promise. An external brand is a promise to the customer. Your corporate culture is a promise to your employees. If either of these fail to deliver on their promise, it will be difficult to compete with speed, quality and innovation, and create loyal, repeat customers.

One of the industries with the biggest disconnect between brand advertising and both customer and employee experience is banking. The ads of Wells Fargo portrayed a brand promise of efficiency, stewardship and a long heritage of service to customers and the community. However, the employee experience, especially at the branch and retail level was anything but. Employees were driven to meet or exceed goals set by managers hungry for bonuses from top management. The end result was fraud and disengaged employees that went on for five years and resulted in $150 million in fines and the resignation of the Chief Executive, and loss of brand integrity.

Want to better align brand and culture? Before it merged with a bigger bank, Corner Bank of Kansas combined marketing and HR under a single senior vice president, thereby putting a strong emphasis on the alignment between brand and culture.[55]

 Advertising is important, the design of the website is important,
but if customers have a positive experience every time they
come into the bank, that's what builds our reputation. We've

got mobile apps, we've got Internet banking, but what we rely on is a hometown feeling. When you walk into our bank, we know your name.
~Jana Dobbs, SVP Marketing and HR, Corner Bank

USAA, based in Austin, Texas, is an insurance and finance company with 11.9 million customers and a net worth of $29 billion. What is unique among large insurers is that USAA employees have a strong emotional connection to their customers, who are all active or retired members of the US military and their families. In fact, they aren't just customers, they are more like family to the company's 21,000 employees.

Because most of its interactions with customers are over the phone or Internet, the company has a world-class customer service training program that not only focuses on technical skills, but also on customer empathy, seeing the world through the eyes and experiences of their members. Soldiers serving abroad have special needs in complicated circumstances, from wiring money to a sick relative to supporting the spouse in financing a car at home. The USAA customer service training even goes so far as having service representatives wear 65-pound military backpacks around the office and eating military ready meals, and reading actual letters from overseas soldiers to their families. At USAA, the culture is the brand, and the brand is the culture.

 We built the Starbucks brand first with our people, not with consumers. The opposite approach from that of the crackers and cereal companies.
~Howard Schultz

Principle Ten:

Leaders and Employees Change Cultures, Not Consultants

 Only the wisest and the stupidest of men never change.
~ Confucious

Culture change is on the minds of many business executives for the simple reason that rapid changes in technology, globalization, increased competition and instant communication have created marketplace conditions that require revised business models, reshaped strategies, new channels to market, and more effective organization structures. Most senior executives realize that to effectively implement and execute on new strategies and structures will require a reshaped culture in alignment with these new approaches.

 Change your opinions, keep your principles.
Change your leaves, keep intact your roots.
~Victor Hugo

And there are a plethora of culture change consultants and firms clamoring to help reshape or change your corporate culture. Most of these firms offer interventions that are centered around proprietary change models and cascading culture change workshops, all of course beginning at the top with the senior team and then cascading downwards. The purpose of this massive undertaking is to engage a critical mass of employees in culture trainings. All this activity is based on the belief that once a critical mass is reached, a significant behavior change will take place as a result.

As established early on in this book, the visible elements of corporate culture (habitual behaviors, ways of working and relating with peers, other departments and customers) are really the outcomes of the corporate culture system, which is composed of multiple culture drivers. Habits and behaviors are difficult to change. It is very difficult to change our personal habitual behavior patterns, and almost impossible to change the behavior of others. And the majority of culture change training is mostly focused on culture information and education and results in little significant change in people or culture.

In an article titled, *Success Rates for Different Types of Organizational Change*, [56] researcher Martin E. Smith compared 49 published reports of successful organizational change, representing over 40,000 organizations and came to an important insight: culture change programs fail much more often than strategy implementations and organization redesign projects. His research states the success rate of real culture change is somewhere around 20%. In 2008, a McKinsey &Co. global survey of 3,199 executives found that only 1/3 of organization transformational efforts succeeded. [57]

By understanding that the visible behaviors people refer to as corporate culture are actually the outcome of the corporate culture system, it is possible to locate the key culture change drivers. Therein lay the leverages for culture change.

 Don't try to change corporate culture,
instead change the drivers of culture.

Reshape the Culture Drivers

Here is an excellent example from the retail healthcare industry. Between 2000 and 2010 the business strategy of the Walgreens Company was based on expanding its retail footprint, with a goal of having 7,000 stores by 2010. To accomplish this fast growth strategy, they created a command and control culture where tasks and processes were clearly laid out, budgets and projects tightly controlled and leaders focused on data to drive store location decisions and management decisions. And it worked. Walgreens went from 4,250 stores in 2003 to 7,000 in 2009.[58]

However, in 2010 the business and competitive landscape began to shift. More competitors entered the pharmacy and subscription filling business, including third-party pharmacy benefits-management companies that deliver prescriptions by mail. Grocery stores started expanding their instore pharmacies, and the Internet players started to push drug and healthcare products. With the passage of the Affordable Care Act, plus the global economic crisis, came a huge focus by customers on improved quality and reduced cost for healthcare service and products.

Walgreens leadership believed there was an opportunity to become a leader in the healthcare value chain by becoming a preferred destination for health and daily-living products, plus healthcare advice and services. To do so Walgreens would have to reshape its strategy from a real estate play with tight processes and command and control leadership, to a strategy of delivering exceptional advisory services and an enhanced customer experience based on friendliness, speed, quality and low cost. To deliver this new strategy required a culture where front-line staff felt empowered, emotionally engaged with a new mission, and devoted to quality healthcare and an exceptional customer experience. Walgreens wanted to become not just a place to have prescriptions filled at low cost, but a destination for quality healthcare support, services, advice and products.

 If employees can get emotionally engaged in serving coffee (like at Starbucks), why can't our employees get engaged in helping people be healthy?
~Mark Wagner and Wayne Orvis, Walgreens

By understanding that corporate culture is an integrated business system, Walgreen leaders realized they had to redesign many of the old culture drivers. Store and frontline leadership and management roles needed to change to allow time for coaching and support for store staff. To accomplish this culture shift they had to reshape management roles and job descriptions, alter compensation formulas to focus on a combination of financials, team management, and customer service, and free up managers from excessive administration requirements with the use of new technology.

They also moved functions like HR, IT, real estate, employee relations and finance from the corporate office into field locations to provide faster support and decision making for the stores. Local merchandising decisions were taken out of the stores and up to regional levels in order to free up store management time to better coach and support staff. In addition, they created the new position of Community Leaders to coach and mentor less experienced store managers in the requirements of the new culture. In addition, roles shifted from staff completing routine tasks to coming up with ideas and new ways of helping and supporting customers. And community engagement became a prime focus for every store to build brand recognition and community spirit.

Walgreen didn't focus on a traditional approach of culture change trainings and cascading workshops to try to change employee behaviors and the culture. They redesigned the drivers within their old corporate culture system and focused on the culture drivers with the most impact: leadership roles and responsibilities, compensation formulas, company policies and work practices, organization design and peer-to-peer coaching. And the results are promising, with employee engagement leaping from the bottom quartile into the 95th percentile. Company financial results in 2013, a year after the shift, were the best in a decade.

A similar story of culture change took place in the mid 1980's at the General Motors Freemont Assembly plant, notorious for being the worst facility for poor quality, frequent Union strikes and work slowdowns. The plant was known for such bad quality that it was not uncommon for workers to put half-eaten tuna sandwiches into the door panels before bolting them shut as a way to getting back at management. And managers hated working there and treated employees with disdain.

Instead of implementing a massive training program to change management and employee behaviors, in 1984 GM and its new partner, Toyota, installed the Toyota Production System. TPS features new roles for managers as coaches and a high level of respect for employees, plus the ability of workers to stop the line at any time so that poor quality could be fixed on the spot (a process known as *Andon*).

In 1985 a Car and Driver magazine headline read: *"When Hell Freezes Over"* (the title alluding to a miracle). The article focused on the culture change at the plant. The Freemont plant had reopened in late 1984 and one year later had the highest quality of any GM automotive plant, absenteeism had fallen from above 20% to less than 2%, not one strike, and all with the same employees! Freemont was producing great cars by great people. For the next 25 years, the NUMMI plant was a showcase of modern management and an example of a high-performance culture.

All successful culture change approaches have two things in common: courageous leadership and employees taking accountability for the culture.

Courage and Accountability

Leadership, that means the CEO and senior leaders at all levels, must do the work required to identify and then change the culture drivers that produce unwanted behaviors. Sadly, too few leaders have that kind of understanding and insight about the corporate culture system. And fewer still have the courage to change the drivers. Consider the global banking industry where the press and regulatory bodies have been screaming about the broken culture of banking, yet leadership has turned a blind eye to the internal culture drivers that promote greed, excessive risk, cover-ups, peer pressure to look the other way, and poor teamwork and transparency.

 It takes a village to raise a child.
It takes all employees to reshape culture.

Culture change is an inside-out job. While leaders can change the drivers, employees at all levels must accept the responsibility for the new culture. And here is where the powerful culture driver of peer-pressure and informal leaders come in. Basically, changes and new ways of working are either promulgated or resisted through an internal social network by key influencers and peer pressure.

The Role of "Informal" Leaders and Key Influencers on Introduction of New Behaviors

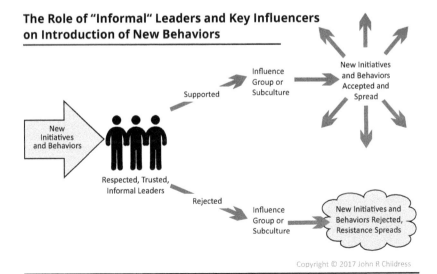

Dr. Leandro Herrero, author of a seminal book on culture and organizations, *Homo Imitans*, had the unique insight that social networks, in conjunction with peer pressure, have a major impact on the development and sustainability of corporate culture.[59] And one particular group of individuals in an organization holds the key to rapid and sustainable culture change.

They are the individuals, from all levels (hourly to executive) that are most trusted and respected by their peers and others in the company. People listen when they speak. People follow and imitate their behaviors, attitudes and points of view about work, management, customer service and culture. They are the trendsetters and the 'informal leaders' with great power to sway opinion and behavior.

Sustainable Culture Change

Beginning a culture change is easy, but spreading, sustaining and maintaining is the hard part. Behavior and attitude changes are adopted, not because of top down proclamations by senior management, but by the role modeling and promoting of change by key-influential individuals. Instead of the top-down push process of most culture change methodologies, real culture change takes hold through a pull effect, a social contagion, a viral social movement, with the support of senior leadership changing the culture drivers that will facilitate the adoption of new behaviors and ways of working.

Real culture change is about new behaviors at scale. An effective safety culture is not measured by the amount of money and time spent on training, but by the everyday use of safe behaviors. And PowerPoint slides or training sessions don't produce new behaviors, at best they introduce and reinforce new information.

Traditional top-down culture change and cascading workshops spread information and a little enthusiasm. With courageous leaders being willing to reshape the culture drivers, and by identifying and engaging key influencers and the internal social network, sustainable culture change will take hold.

 Never doubt that a small group of thoughtful, committed citizens can change the world; indeed, it's the only thing that ever does. ~Margaret Mead

Section Two

Leveraging Corporate Culture for Business Success

Leveraging Corporate Culture for Business Success

❝❞ *Give me a lever long enough and a fulcrum on which to place it, and I shall move the world. ~Archimedes*

Archimedes was an ancient Greek mathematician, physicist, engineer, inventor, and astronomer who lived from 287 BC – 212 B.C. With just a few principles of hydraulics and mathematics, Archimedes used his knowledge to solve a number of challenging problems, such as how to tell if an object was pure gold or a mixture of metals. He also invented a machine to move water from one place to another which became known as Archimedes Screw. He even used his knowledge to lift massive warships completely out of the water. In essence, he was an early applications engineer.

My goal in this book is bigger than simply describing the core principles behind corporate culture. What is more important is to help the reader use this understanding and knowledge to build better organizations that can deliver sustainable value for all stakeholders.

Applied appropriately, these core principles can improve strategy execution, increase employee engagement, create competitive advantage, reduce workplace stress, improve productivity, foster innovation and increase market value. Corporate culture is much more than a concept; it is a critical business system and a major lever for economic and social improvement.

 I came to see, in my time at IBM, that culture isn't just one aspect of the game, it is the game. In the end, an organization is nothing more than the collective capacity of its people to create value. – Louis Gerstner, IBM

There are many business issues and challenges where the application of the principles of corporate culture can be of great value. In the following chapters I will touch on a few of the most common I have encountered during my client advisory work.

These scenarios include:

- o   The New Leader and Corporate Culture
- o   Corporate Culture and Strategy Execution
- o   Going for Growth
- o   The Start Up: Getting the Culture Right from the Beginning
- o   Culture and M&A
- o   Delivering a Sustainable Turnaround
- o   Corporate Culture and Leadership Development
- o   Culture and Values
- o   Culture and the Customer
- o   Culture and Middle Management
- o   Culture and Employee Engagement
- o   A Culture for Innovation
- o   Culture and Technology
- o   Corporate Culture and the Board
- o   Building a "Global" Corporate Culture
- o   Building a Future-Proof Culture

With each situation I will show how one or more of the core principles of corporate culture can help improve business performance and organizational health.

The New Leader and Corporate Culture

 I have been a stranger in a strange land.
~Moses

Imagine parachuting into a strange city in a foreign country where the language and customs are different and you don't have an illustrated travel book to help make sense of your new surroundings. And on top of that, you aren't just a tourist, you are their new leader and expected to slay the monsters outside the city walls. You and I can wake up from this nightmare scenario, but the new leader can't. This is their new life.

The challenges facing the new leader are numerous and few new CEOs or team leaders are adequately prepared for everything they will encounter in their new role. They may have been highly successful in their former company. Many have been in senor leadership positions before in another company. Yet the reality is, no two companies are the same, and what worked well at one company may not work at their new one.

 All corporate cultures are built from the same core principles,
but not all cultures are the same.

With all the challenges facing the new CEO or senior executive, it is no wonder the failure rate is so high. Research by Heidrick & Struggles, one of the top global retained executive search firms, suggests that between

40-50% of newly hired executives leave an organization within 18 months of hiring,[60] and the financial and lost opportunity costs to the company can be upwards of ten times their salary, not to mention the potential market missteps that often occur with short tenure leaders.

Many new leaders, with an eagerness to prove themselves and to quickly make a positive impact, unwittingly set themselves up for failure by not recognizing the uniqueness of the company, the competitive landscape, or the culture.[61] Some of the common pitfalls new leaders make are:

- o Coming in with a pre-prepared strategy.
- o Immediately proposing new values and vision.
- o Not seeking input from customers and suppliers.
- o Making big decisions too quickly.
- o Spending too much time comparing the new company to their old one.
- o Prioritizing the input of recently-hired team members over incumbents.
- o Not listening to insiders or asking for help.
- o Believing the company works the same way as their previous company.

I was invited by a new CEO to talk about his challenges and opportunities. He was only 3 months into his new role and already a little frustrated. When I arrived at the company offices he was engaged with a customer problem and instructed one of his VPs to give me a tour of the facility.

As we were walking down a long hallway towards one of the assembly areas, the door at the far end opened and another VP entered. Immediately my guide pulled me through an open doorway and into a large meeting room, saying in a hushed tone, *"Let's stay in here for a few minutes, I can't stand that SOB!"*

Sitting with the new CEO later that day he said to me, *"There doesn't seem to be a culture of teamwork at this place. The departments just won't work together or share information. It's like they are at war with each other. Teamwork and sharing information was easy at my last company".*

I asked him why he thought that was the case and got a blank stare. I then related the incident of the two executives earlier in the day and shared with him the shadow of the leader principle. *"When two senior executives are at war with each other, why would you expect their respective departments to get along? Your senior team probably displays multiple bad behaviors on a recurring basis, which are interpreted by managers and employees as acceptable behavior, and a way to stay on the boss' good side. If one VP consistently blames and berates another department, you can forget about teamwork between their functions!"*

The implications were immediately obvious and the CEO replied, *"They do argue a lot, even in staff meetings, but in my other company senior executives were expected to debate things openly to get to the best answers. It was just part of the culture and everyone knew it. But I never connected the dots that such behavior in this company is seen very differently and how it negatively impacts the company and performance".*

To this CEO's credit, over the next few weeks he had one-on-one meetings with every member of the senior team to talk about acceptable and non-acceptable behavior, and how to argue about issues in order to get the best solution without making it personal. Most quickly understood and began to manage their individual and collective behavior. A few needed additional coaching from their peers and one was asked by the CEO to leave the company. With a new set of behavioral norms coming from the top, teamwork and cross-functional cooperation started to become a part of the corporate culture.

 One thing we've talked a lot about, even in the first leadership meeting, was what's the purpose of our leadership team? The framework we came up with is the notion that our purpose is to bring clarity, alignment and intensity. ~Satya Nadella, CEO Microsoft

Digging Into the Culture

One of the quickest ways for a new CEO to learn about the strengths and weaknesses of their new company culture is to talk with suppliers and customers. If it is a retail company, become a mystery shopper for a day. Call the customer service hotline with questions or problems to see how they react. Search out and speak with former executives who have moved on. Have the secretaries make a list of all the standing meetings and their frequency. Find out how many meetings the members of your senior team attend in a week, and how much or how little thinking time the executives have.

As a new leader, you could even go on a culture hunt. Wander around the office and look into cubicles to see what kinds of cartoons and sayings you find pinned up. One private equity company I know about has a rule that if they find a plethora of cynical Dilbert cartoons in cubicles they tend to back away from a potential investment or purchase. Read the graffiti on the bathroom stalls. Come in on the third shift to watch the activity and how people behave. Have a drink at the bars your employees tend to frequent and listen to the talk.

There are many culture elements you can discover through judicious observation. Is there a pattern to how the parking lots fill up and empty, and is there preferred parking for executives or guests? What are the company rituals? Are there any Hero and Bum stories that new employees quickly learn about? Is there signage up in the halls promoting the company, customers and products, or just random pictures? Do executives eat lunch in their offices or head to the cafeteria and interact with employees? Check the personnel records and see why employees were terminated in the past 3 years. How much effort and time is put into employee onboarding and training? Do customers ever come and speak to employees about how they use their products and service?

Data from a McKinsey & Co. study of roughly 600 chief executives at S&P 500 companies between 2004 and 2014, suggests that the new CEOs who produced greater than 500% growth in shareholder returns in their new company were about equally split between insiders and outsiders. [62] Whether or not the CEO is an internal hire or external, the first step in navigating the new role successfully is to cultivate an outsider's viewpoint in order to challenge everything, especially the cultural norms and attitudes about how things are done.

Time to Decompress

Any new CEO or executive hire should make time for quiet reflection and thinking. In too many cases, a newly hired executive is thrown into a marathon of internal and external meetings, with little time devoted to reflection, assimilation and synthesis of information.

Those in senior leadership positions, especially new hires, function almost constantly in a high pressure environment. They start early in the morning with phone calls to staff in locations around the globe, then race from meeting to meeting with little time in between, more conference calls, lunch with clients or analysts, more meetings, a dash to the airport, usually a conference call once they reach the hotel late at night, a few hours of sleep, and the treadmill starts again early the next morning with a client breakfast and a full day of more meetings before it's back to the airport. The phone calls and emails usually keep coming even on the weekend.

New hires in senior roles need to decompress regularly or run the risk of making poor decisions. If new leaders don't take the time to decompress, that is to have regular, uninterrupted thinking time, time for reflection, time for forward planning and to explore multiple options without time pressures, even good executives will eventually make poor decisions.

 The reality is that important decisions made by intelligent, responsible people with the best information and intentions are sometimes hopelessly flawed.
~Professor Sidney Finkelstein

Most decisions in business are a product of information analysis, pattern recognition based on past experiences, and emotional attachments.[63] These three ingredients often ensure quick and appropriate decisions. However, when a leader is stressed and under pressure, the objective analysis often gets little attention due to time pressures and past patterns and emotional attachments take the lead. Under pressure and stress, past patterns and emotional attachments get distorted and stretched out of shape. Thus it is not uncommon for good leaders to make bad decisions.

I have found that most business executives and leaders fail to fully understand or appreciate the need for decompression time in which they can sort out competing agendas and conflicting information. Most of their diaries are controlled by others, with little time for reflection and thinking, thus the over-reliance on pattern recognition and emotional triggers. The solution is for the new leader to take control of their calendar and diary and purposefully schedule daily time for decompression stops.

Time is the enemy of the new CEO. And of all people the new CEO does not have the luxury of time to dig in fully, explore all the loose ends, and most importantly, think! There are various estimates by academics on just what the grace period is for a new CEO. Some say six months, some 100 days, some 3 months before the new CEO must produce a solid assessment and most importantly, a workable go-forward plan. But on one thing everyone agrees, in the past few years the grace period has gotten shorter and shorter.

The New CEO's Secret Weapon

There is, however, a secret weapon in the arsenal of the new CEO. That weapon is an understanding of the leadership culture. The culture at the top, one of the most influential subcultures in the entire organization, has a great influence on all aspects of the business, from strategy execution to company pride and teamwork. The problem with understanding leadership culture is that it is mostly invisible, and with a new CEO on board, many members of the senior team are on their best behavior.

The quickest way to get a handle on the leadership subculture is to get the entire senior team together at a 3 or 4 day away meeting during the first month. One day is not enough time for executives to show their real character, 3-4 days is best. This meeting should be custom designed for your company and facilitated by an external person, perhaps an advisor or colleague the CEO has used in the past. Besides some revealing team building exercises, this meeting's agenda should contain mostly activities run by the team members themselves. All attendees should come prepared to debate key business and cultural questions, such as:

- o What is the corporate culture of this company? How do you know?
- o How does our culture either propel or hinder business results?
- o What are our shared objectives as a leadership team?
- o What are the critical few breakthrough objectives we should be focusing on to grow this business, better service customers, and beat the competition?
- o What are the fewest metrics we need to run this business properly?
- o What projects/programs do we need to deliver on our strategic agenda?
- o What projects/programs are running that don't fit this agenda?
- o Who is going to be accountable for what?

The new CEO should not lead these discussions, but participate as a member of the team, and watch the behaviors of individuals and of the group. Pay attention to who dominates the discussions, who keeps silent, who is fully engaged and who keeps sneaking a look at their emails. With careful observation, you will soon learn who supports and encourages open discussion, who uses an aggressive personality to hammer others into submission, who (if anyone) talks about the customer, who is an optimist, and who is a cynic. People reveal more of their real personalities and leadership habits in a group situation than during a 1-on-1 meeting.

In just 3 days you will quickly learn the type of leadership culture you have inherited. And you will also quickly discover who's on the bus and who isn't. You will also learn a lot about the business from the people who "should" know the most. Also look for those who bring facts and data to the discussion and those who try to persuade through "my personal experience".

It is also important to follow-up after the workshop with 1-on-1 conversations with each member of the team to learn more about how they see the company and the team. In short order you will have more insight into the leadership team, the corporate culture, and the business than if you spent the next 6 months sitting through endless meetings and hundreds of PowerPoint presentations.

When a new leader decides to make some changes at the top, remember to take advantage of the culture principle that stories about who gets fired and who gets promoted are strong culture drivers. If someone in a senior position needs to be terminated don't let HR or legal put out a whitewash email message when you can instead use the power of culture to send a strong message to the entire company. People should know directly from the CEO what is acceptable and encouraged in terms of manager and employee behavior, what capabilities the company needs in order to gain competitive advantage and how poor teamwork or building individual fiefdoms will not be tolerated. This can be done without talking about the terminated individual at all, but everyone needs to understand that corporate culture is a non-negotiable.

 If I were running a company today, I would have one priority above all others: to acquire as many of the best people as I could. I'd put off everything else to fill my bus. Because things are going to come back. My flywheel is going to start to turn. And the single biggest constraint on the success of my organization is the ability to get and to hang on to enough of the right people. ~Jim Collins

Corporate Culture
and Strategy Execution

 *The important thing is not having a strategy,
it's getting it executed.* ~Jack Welch

I doubt if there are many business executives in the world who haven't read Clayton Christensen's seminal study on disruptive strategies and the case study of Nucor specialty steel mills.[64] When Nucor was founded, the steel industry had been long dominated by large, vertically integrated mega-mills who kept acquiring other mills under the strategy that size brings economy of scale, helps reduce product costs and increases competitiveness. This was the standard wisdom in the steel industry and resulted in a market dominated by a few large American companies such as US Steel, Bethlehem Steel and Republic. To achieve greater efficiency of scale they systematically abandoned specialty steels as being low volume and too expensive.

Seeing that small could be profitable with the right business model and the right culture, Nucor bought a small mill in 1967 and began turning out the specialty steels which were no longer easily available from the big steel makers. As they grew and became more profitable at the lower end of the market, Nucor then began making other steels that the big mills were dropping in their search for economy of scale. In a few decades, Nucor became the largest and most profitable steel producer in North America, having achieved more than 160 consecutive quarters of dividends and the highest return to shareholders of any company in the Standard & Poor's 500 between 2004 and 2009.

What's even more interesting about the success of Nucor is the role played by its own unique corporate culture. The Nucor Culture [65] has five core elements:

- o Decentralized management
- o Performance based compensation
- o Egalitarian benefits
- o Customer service and quality
- o Technological leadership

Underlying these elements is the fact that none of Nucor's plants, whether built from scratch or acquired, is unionized. The company has never laid off an employee due to a work shortage. The Nucor culture is a competitive advantage and a significant aid in the effective execution of its business strategy. In 2017 Nucor ranked 26th out of the 500 best employers to work for in America by Forbes[66]. Ken Iverson, the former CEO and Chairman, attributes 30% of the company's success to technology and innovation, and 70% to its unique corporate culture.

When culture and strategy are aligned, it has a positive impact on strategy execution. According to a recent study by Korn-Ferry, 72% of executives say culture is extremely important for organizational performance, yet only 32% of executives believe their organization's culture is fully aligned with the business strategy.[67]

Aligning Culture and Strategy

One of the ways to better align culture and strategy for effective execution is to clearly define the specific work behaviors and culture drivers required to deliver your strategy. These should not be platitudes, but specific workplace actions, internal processes, policies and employee behaviors that are easy for employees to understand and follow, not only at the executive level, but down to the department and team level. If you can take your overall company strategy and recast it into daily work behaviors and business processes, the culture will move towards alignment with the strategy, which is one of the key requirements for effective strategy execution.

 There is no strategy without execution.

In 2003, Lycoming Engine Co. lost a major portion of its 80% market share following a failed outsourcing strategy that led to faulty crankshafts in their airplane engines, resulting in multiple lawsuits. To engineer a sustainable turnaround plus rebuild pride and morale, the new senior team realized that it could only effectively execute on its new turnaround strategy if every employee understood the entire strategy, their role, plus the team and individual behaviors required. With long term employees who understood the importance of quality and safety, engagement would be a major factor in moving the company from near bankruptcy to industry leadership.

To engage employees and make the turnaround strategy easy to understand, the senior team developed a visual strategy dashboard that not only had metrics, which were regularly updated, but also specific attitudes and behaviors for each strategic objective in the turnaround plan. Posters were placed on every work cell message board on the manufacturing floor and in every conference room. At the beginning of every meeting, no matter what the issue or level of attendees, the first agenda item was reminding everyone of the Lycoming 2004 Priorities. The company also held a series of culture workshops with the theme of *"Back to the Future"* to capture the best of the previous culture while adding in new culture drivers focused around lean manufacturing principles, 5-S methodologies, transparent communications and improved supervisor training.

Today, Lycoming Engine Company is again the premier maker of engines for the single engine aviation and sport racing market, with their innovative race engines powering the Red Bull Air Aces stunt and race teams. They recently won the North American Shingo Prize for Operational Excellence, a far cry from their near bankruptcy days.

Major studies by academics and consulting firms estimate that between 55-70% of strategic plans fail to deliver on their stated business objectives. In a 2008 McKinsey & Co. study of 197 companies, despite 97% of directors believing they had the right strategic vision and plan, only 33% responded that they achieved significant strategic success. [68] In some strategy failures, management fails to take into account technology or market changes, while other failures are caused by a lack of adequate funding. However, most experts agree that a major reason for the high failure rate of strategy execution is corporate culture being out of alignment with the requirements of the business strategy.

For example, if your strategy is highly dependent upon customer loyalty for service and spare parts revenue, but your Parts department and field salesforce aren't linked through shared objectives, it will be difficult to meet spare parts availability and service promises. As a result, customers will naturally seek other avenues for repairs and service and even begin shopping around for non-branded parts. In a case like this, speed of parts delivery and quick-response service is critical when customer machines are inoperable and equipment downtime is vital to their profitability.

To better align strategy and culture, it is important to focus your culture around critical, cross-functional value chains instead of around individual department budgets. In the example of the parts and service departments above, the Trouble-to-Resolve value chain maps out all the functions, information exchanges and handoffs that occur from the time a customer reports a problem to its final resolution. In many cases you will find significant wasted time as information and requirements are passed from one department to another, not because employees don't want to help the customer, but because their objectives and work practices focus on functional goals, not the overall customer-centric strategy. This is a clear example of the culture drivers of budgets, compensation and organization design being out of alignment with the strategic objective of superior customer service and enduring customer loyalty.

 In my experience, business success is 15% strategy, 50% execution, 35% culture. An outstanding strategy weakly executed will always be trumped by a weak strategy with outstanding execution. Culture is a key part of execution. If the strategy or execution conflict with the culture, bet on the culture. ~Bob Legge

For a more in-depth exploration of the importance of corporate culture and leadership on effective strategy execution, see *FASTBREAK: The CEO's Guide to Strategy Execution.* [135]

Going for Growth

▌▌ *Firms need to ensure that their ability to provide effective customer service keeps pace with their growth.*
~Arthur Levitt, Former Chairman of the U.S. Securities and Exchange Commission

Growth is the holy grail of almost every business. Growth brings in revenue and attracts investor money which in turn can be used to develop new products, service and support more customers, deliver bonuses and improved employee benefits, reward owners, investors and shareholders, and increase market value. However, only 11% of companies manage to grow profits and revenues by just 5.5% or more over a 10-year period.[69] Growth is desired, but not guaranteed.

There are many organizational and leadership challenges facing companies which manage to grow and expand. Rapid growth can easily outstrip the internal capabilities of company systems and service platforms, or overstretch employees with added workloads. In most cases, rapid growth and business success eventually leads to a company crisis. The internal systems and culture can't keep up with the escalating demands of the business.

A longitudinal study by Bain & Company found that 94% of executives who led companies with revenues greater than $5 billion said that internal issues, not external ones, kept their companies from growing profitably[69]. The primary internal barriers to growth were identified as revenues growing faster than talent, complexity of decision making, less contact with and understanding of customer needs, internal leadership conflicts about direction and strategy, and difficulty mobilizing resources. All of these challenges increase with growth. Growth creates complexity, and complexity is the invisible derailer of profitability.

Below is a chart showing the revenue history of a company from its early days in the 1920's as a regional supplier of equipment and services to its current status as a global leader in its industry. The history of innovation and customer service of this privately held, family-owned company is impressive, but its explosive growth created unforeseen problems.

Revenue History

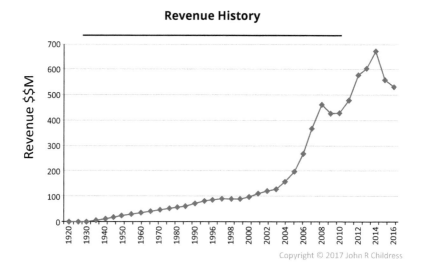

The revenue downturn in 2015 and 2016 reflects an economic slowdown that impacted their industry. Under such conditions, many companies seek to reduce costs through headcount reductions and by delaying investments. While declining revenue might be explained by external market conditions, this one-factor explanation runs the risk of overlooking internal organizational issues as ancillary causal factors.

In many companies experiencing significant growth, employee head count increases consistently during the boom years. In one organization, by the time a downturn occurred, 59% of employees had been hired within the last 4 years. And these new employees came from different companies which had very different corporate cultures.

In such a situation, on-boarding and hiring profiles are two important culture drivers. In many growth companies these drivers are often developed without thought to the impact new employees have on the current corporate culture. When a large number of new employees come from companies with different cultures, cultural dilution and fragmentation can be significant.

When a company's original culture is informal and new employee on-boarding minimal, it is left to each new hire to determine, on their own, what is expected in terms of workplace behaviors and how to deal with customers. The end result is almost always a significant dilution of the old culture to such an extent that teamwork, open communications and trust can be significantly eroded.

With an on-boarding process based on intranet documents and self-directed study designed to be efficient and save costs, new employees in the field and those in support functions can behave more like strangers than teammates, without shared values and with weak bonds of trust and respect. Service and customer support can quickly suffer and in some cases can even negatively impact innovation and the new product development process.

 You can't build a great building on a weak foundation. You must have a solid foundation if you're going to have a strong superstructure. ~Gordon B. Hinckley

Scaling Corporate Culture

Not all company policies and business processes scale; not all corporate cultures scale, either. Informal cultures based on everyone knowing each other quickly reach a point where they are no longer effective at supporting the business. The growth and demise of Nortel Networks, which at one time accounted for more than a third of the total valuation of all the companies listed on the Toronto Stock Exchange (TSX) and employed 94,500 people worldwide, is a prime example.

Nortel was the poster child for technology applications in the early years of telecommunications and digital networks, and the first company in its industry to deliver a complete line of fully digital telecommunications products. Starting in 1977, Nortel grew rapidly after the introduction of its DMS line of digital central office telephone switches, especially after the AT&T breakup in 1984. Nortel became a significant supplier in Europe and China and was the first non-Japanese supplier to Nippon Telegraph and Telephone (NTT).

However, in January 14, 2009, Nortel filed for bankruptcy protection from its creditors in the United States, Canada, and the United Kingdom. In June 2009, the company announced it would cease operations and sell off all of its business units. Nortel, once the high flyer in a sexy and lucrative industry, died an inglorious and painful death.

What is fascinating about the Nortel story is the role played by corporate culture. For much of its early life the Nortel culture could be described as a *"large family"* where everyone knew each other, knew how things worked and knew who to call if they needed any support on a deal, information for a sales pitch or help in resolving a customer problem. Issues got resolved quickly through the informal organization and Nortel's speed to market with new products and services was a significant competitive advantage.

According to Gary Donahee, one of the key senior leaders during the explosive growth of Nortel: *"we knew who the good guys were and just gave them a call when we really needed to get something accomplished, and it worked well".*[7] Most employees during that time agreed that Nortel's high-performance, informal culture focused on sales and service was strong.

With a desire to grow quickly, Nortel hired hundreds and hundreds of new managers, executives and employees who knew the official organization chart, but not the informal organization. Naturally, these new hires came with their own set of behaviors and attitudes about business and management. This rapid influx of outsiders, although they had the necessary experience and skills, diluted the original Nortel culture until it became inconsistent and unfocused. The strong informal culture of getting things done quickly had been watered down. Nortel became a large, global organization, but had little cohesion around behaviors and attitudes towards work, customers and team members.

As a result, decision-making slowed down. Getting something through the system became more and more difficult until Nortel began losing ground to more agile companies. When this happened, a significant number of experienced senior executives cashed in their stock options and retired. Nortel limped along, finally filed for bankruptcy, and subsequently died. When Nortel outgrew its original culture, it wound up with a weak and fractionated corporate culture full of subcultures and conflicting views on everything from customer service to business ethics.

Recent research on Silicon Valley companies has shown a strong connection between sustainable growth and culture.[70] The study particularly pointed out six behaviors which characterize adaptive corporate cultures:

- o   Risk-taking
- o   A willingness to experiment
- o   Innovation
- o   Personal initiative
- o   Fast decision-making and execution
- o   Ability to spot unique opportunities

As we know from our understanding of corporate culture as a business system, these so called adaptive behaviors are really the outcomes of specific culture drivers, such as internal policies, work processes, recognition systems and reinforcement by leadership. To the above list I would personally add hiring profiles and on-boarding as critical to building a culture of adaptability.

The search for growth may mean creating a new business unit with a completely different culture in order to give it an opportunity to grow successfully. Consider the case of a suburban retail chain that decided to expand into more urban areas.[71] They could have used the same business model, same supply chains, same store fixtures, same hiring profiles and same HR policies. Instead they chose to create a separate business unit. The senior leaders recognized that the business models and customer base for urban versus suburban stores were different. Cost structures needed to be different, as did the corporate cultures.

   Corporate culture is not an initiative; it is the internal corporate culture system that either supports or derails all initiatives.

The Start Up:
Getting the Culture Right from the Beginning

 I think company culture is something you breathe every day, not a slide deck you receive the first day you arrive.
~ Massimo Chieruzzi, AdEspresso

Start-up companies have a precarious early childhood and most don't survive into their teen years. It is difficult to work through cash flow pressures, longer than necessary product development cycles and trying to read the tea leaves of changing customer requirements. Getting everyone to focus on a few critical issues is often challenging in a high-energy start-up since everyone is excited about creating new things. Start-ups are often long on ideas and short on focus. Even if a start-up does get the product-market mix right and have adequate backing, creating a culture that will scale takes additional work and time.

Two successful start-ups that took the time to codify their corporate culture early on and use it as a platform for business success were Netflix and Hubspot, fast growing consumer-centric technology companies that now are global leaders in their field.

 Let's make the company we always dreamed of.
Let's create a company that will be a great place to be from.
~Reed Hastings and Patty McCord, Netflix

The founders of Netflix, the online video streaming and content

---

production mega-business, recognized culture was the foundation for building, scaling and sustaining their business. Their culture document, a 126-page PowerPoint deck, became their *de facto* business plan against which all decisions were evaluated. The Netflix culture deck, published on the web as *Netflix Culture, Freedom and Responsibility*,[72] has over 6 million views. Sheryl Sandberg, former COO of Facebook, called it *"the most important document ever to come out of Silicon Valley"*.

Culture By Design

The *Netflix Culture* document is important because it is among the first and clearest articulations of the elements of a corporate culture system by design. In contrast to a default culture, a designed culture addresses several critical elements in building a competitive and sustainable organization. For Netflix, these elements include:

- o   Why a clear and well understood culture is important today and tomorrow,
- o   Who is expected to lead and promulgate the culture,
- o   Who it is intended to embrace,
- o   What it will mean in terms of aligned actions by all employees,
- o   When cultural change efforts should be made
- o   How cultural changes will be introduced, enabled, enforced, monitored and celebrated.

It is not the culture deck itself, but the effort put in by all employees to build and maintain an aligned corporate culture. Behind each of the seven Netflix cultural values lies not only a rationale but also clear descriptions of behavioral expectations for all employees. While many executives in traditional organizations tend to dismiss such culture decks as a manifesto to Generation Y, used effectively they are powerful in establishing cultural norms from the beginning in order to drive sustainable growth.

The Hubspot Culture Code is a 120-plus page deck describing in detail the company culture, and is a perpetual work in progress that gets updated periodically. They are now on Version 16 of their culture deck as the company has grown to 12,000 customers and over 700 people since its founding in 2005.

The success and growth of Hubspot is impressive, but it was only able to happen because the founders treated corporate culture as a critical business system.

Culture remains central to other start-up companies as well. At Amazon, culture works because it is owned by the employees, not just management or the CEO. Amazon's 14 Leadership Principles are used not only for new employee induction, but also during every product or customer discussion and in all management meetings.[73]

Sustainable Start-Up Cultures

If you want to use culture from the beginning as one of the platforms for ensuring the success of a start up, then here are a few hints gleaned from companies who have successfully navigated from start-up to a high value sustainable business.

Freebies do not equate to corporate culture. Free food and other perks are good at attracting people, but have little to do with innovation, productivity or the retention of real talent. Instead, base your culture on knowledge and continuous learning, which will not only help you attract, but also keep great talent. People want to learn and continuous learning is a big part of a high performance culture. Personal development includes exposing people to new projects, new technologies, new markets and new industries. Challenge your people to keep learning and you will most likely keep them.

Don't think your culture work is done just because you wrote a culture deck and have a culture on-boarding program. Culture is a living system and must be cared for, pruned occasionally, fed and watered regularly, and every once in a while, reshaped to fit the size of the company and the marketplace demands.

While everyone is accountable for maintaining the ascribed culture, a culture team, made up of passionate volunteers and even a few cynics, will pay attention to the culture better than founders and senior executives can. Make a place on the culture team a coveted company position with lots of recognition and acknowledgement. And listen to their input. You may not agree with or like hearing everything they tell you about the current culture, but a toxic culture can spread like a virus and the only antidote is open dialogue and the courage to change.

Find and perpetuate Hero and Bum stories that describe the culture and success in human terms. Make certain these stories feature heavy in recruiting and interviews of potential employees. Some companies even have annual awards based on Hero stories as a way of bringing the culture to life.

Quickly terminate those who openly resist the cultural behaviors desired. If someone is a healthy sceptic, put them on the culture team. You need honest input if you are serious about culture as a business advantage. If they are an unhealthy or toxic sceptic, understand that they will unintentionally infect others with their negativity. After all, no company is perfect and no culture is ideal. You are looking for ideas for continuous improvement from people who care, not those who just want to expose problems.

Finally, make Company Culture a budget line item on your P&L so that it gets properly funded. Attach metrics to your culture budget items. Also, make Corporate Culture one of the key pillars of your formal business strategy. What goes into the written strategic document usually gets funded and delivered.

 In our early years, we didn't talk about culture much. We hadn't documented it all. We just built a business that we wanted to work in. And, that was great. But the real return on culture happened when we started getting more deliberate about it. By writing it down. By debating it. By taking it apart, polishing the pieces and putting it back together. Iterating. Again. And again. ~Dharmesh Shah, Co-founder, Hubspot

Culture and M&A

❝ M&A proposals should come with a health warning:
Acquisitions can result in serious damage to your corporate
health, including death.

Founded in 1762, Barings was the oldest and most prestigious merchant bank in Britain. It financed the Napoleonic wars, the Louisiana Purchase, and the Erie Canal. Barings was the Queen's bank. Yet in 1995 it collapsed and was sold for £1 to a Dutch Bank, ING. While the 233-year-old Barings was brought down single-handedly by a derivatives trader making unauthorized and high risk trades, the seeds of its destruction began in 1984 when Barings, a merchant bank, acquired a small securities trading firm, Henderson Crosthwaite, which was later renamed Barings Securities Limited. This acquisition led to a significant shift in the conservative Barings culture and the ultimate downfall of the bank.

Securities brokers and traders tend to have loud and outgoing personalities and life styles much different from traditional merchant bankers. The brokers' brightly colored suspenders and loud ties were the symbols of a high-risk culture with a preference for short-term profit making. The traders were highly focused on the deal of today, and cared less for developing long term relationships with clients. By contrast, Barings' merchant bankers lived in a gentlemanly culture advising long-term clients on corporate mergers and takeovers.

After a short honeymoon period, internal conflict began between the banking division, which was losing money, and the brokerage division which was making six times as much as the banking division was losing. In contrast to the structured controls inherent in traditional merchant banking, the securities firm was a loosely-controlled operation which valued sales skills and aggressive behavior over compliance and controls.[74,75] The traders began to demand greater autonomy and less management oversight from London in order to remain competitive and make money. At Barings, the squeaky wheel got the grease: internal controls were loosened and Barings management turned a blind eye to the goings on in their brokerage division. After all, they were making huge profits for the bank. A conservative culture of stewardship morphed into a culture of risk and greed.

Nick Leeson, who spent two years at Morgan Stanley as a young operations assistant, joined Barings in London in the late 1980s and worked his way up to the trading floor. In 1990 he was sent to the Singapore office as a manager and through hard work and bravado worked his way into derivatives trading, as well as the senior manager overseeing both front and back offices. Leeson made unauthorized speculative trades that at first made huge profit contributions for Barings.

In 1993 his trades contributed 10% of the total profits of the bank. He became a star within the organization, earning unlimited trust from his London bosses, who considered him nearly infallible. However, his risky trades soon began to lose money, the fact of which he hid in settlement accounts that were not thoroughly scrutinized due to the loose control culture that had taken over at the bank. Finally, to hide mounting losses he took a $7 billion futures position on the Nikkei Stock Exchange that went sour. Barings bank was bankrupt and collapsed.

Yes, it was Leeson who made the undocumented and extremely risky trades, but the culture of loose controls and minimal management oversight at Barings is what allowed it to happen. Looking at a merger or integration based on the balance sheet or strategic synergies and ignoring the potential culture clash can be a recipe for disaster.

M&A Culture Clash

An analysis conducted in 2016 of 2,500 M&A deals shows more than 60% of them actually wind up destroying shareholder value.[76] Even the big firms get it wrong, as we can see in the disastrous results of the Daimler-Chrysler so-called *"merger of equals"*, or the poor results from the combinations of AOL–Time Warner, HP-Compaq and Quaker-Snapple. The only real winners were the advisors who collected fees. Shareholders, employees and customers lost.

In a Bain survey of executives who have managed through mergers, culture clash was the number one reason for failure to deliver promised synergies or value creation.[77] With a clash of cultures, fundamental ways of working are so different and so easily misinterpreted that employees feel frustrated, leading to demoralization, defections and an overall drop in productivity.

 Every single time you make a merger, somebody is losing his identity. And saying something different is just rubbish.
~Carlos Ghosn

With an understanding of corporate culture and some pre-acquisition planning, however, a merger can actually create significant value. Textron Systems Companies (TSC) make, among other things, smart munitions and military Armored Security Vehicles (ASVs) that have a greater survivability probability than the traditional military version Hummer vehicles. Specially designed hull angles and blast resistant plating, along with heavy duty axles, have saved hundreds of lives of coalition forces against landmines and Improvised Explosive Devices (IEDs).

To expand its portfolio of products, Textron Systems spent $600 million in 2007 to acquire AAI, a division of United Industrial Corporation. AAI was a maker of reconnaissance drones (UAVs) for battlefield surveillance and target acquisition, and their products and engineering expertise fit perfectly into Textron's Intelligent Battlefield strategy. Additionally, both companies were based in New England. The financials worked, the product portfolios worked, they were not far apart geographically, and the price was right for both parties. On paper, everything seemed to fit together perfectly.

Textron Systems Company CEO Frank Tempesta wanted to make certain there were no hidden landmines in the deal, especially since this was a major acquisition and historically TSC had a relatively poor M&A record. *"While the numbers added up and AAI was by all accounts a perfect fit for our long term business strategy"*, Tempesta said in an interview about the merger, *"I was concerned about how we were going to integrate such a large number of AAI employees into the Textron family and what that influx would do to our own culture".*

Once the deal was ready to move forward, Tempesta commissioned a custom-developed culture assessment of both organizations to be run alongside the normal integration activities. The survey was designed to illuminate the behaviors and work practices of planning, goal setting, communicating, leading, training and measuring performance. This data was combined with insights gathered from face-to-face and telephone interviews with employees at all levels, so the transition team could gain a more in-depth understanding of both cultures.

What emerged, in as little as two weeks from start to finish, was a graphical snapshot of the differences and similarities of the two company cultures, which showed visually some key culture integration issues that had previously been unrecognized. As it turned out, several significant cultural differences posed a potential risk for the success of the integration.

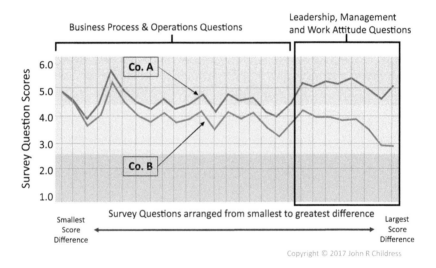

If you just evaluate the business process and operational elements of the two companies, they look like a pretty good fit. This is the typical approach during due diligence. However, there were significant cultural differences notable between the two companies' leadership and management styles, as well as employee attitudes about work.

During a presentation to the senior teams of both TSC and AAI, the information from the Culture Due-Diligence Assessment sparked a lively debate that resulted in a number of key actions that had not previously been in the integration plans, including reviewing and adopting some key best practices of AAI across the entire Textron Systems family of companies, a revised senior team configuration, as well as dramatically expanding integration communications.

The information from the culture survey took Ellen Lord, then in charge of the merger integration team by surprise. *"It pointed out, in a very visual way, the areas that we had overlooked in our traditional integration assessment. But it didn't take us long to plug this new information into our plans"*, she said.

AAI was quickly integrated into the TSC family of companies and the acquisition, in the first year, generated new business opportunities where the two organizations were able to combine their strengths to win significant new US Department of Defense contracts.

M&A Culture Insights

One of the best ways to ensure an acquisition delivers real added value is to use an in-depth understanding of the cultures of both companies as a guide on how to approach the integration. When the internal ways of working and cultures are similar, it can make sense to use an assimilation strategy for the integration.

When the cultures are very different, yet there is a good strategic or business rationale for joining forces, there is the option of allowing the newly-acquired company to maintain its own identity as trust and understanding of the people and their capabilities are built slowly and the new leadership team learns how best to leverage the new acquisition for the benefit of everyone.

The successful Disney acquisition of Pixar is a great example. Disney CEO Robert Igor stated: *"There is an assumption in the corporate world that you need to integrate swiftly. My philosophy is exactly the opposite. You need to be respectful and patient"*. His patience and respect paid off in Pixar's continuing success.

Another good example is the acquisition of Zappos.com by Amazon. Although they were acquired in 2009, Zappos.com has been left alone to grow and develop, and it sometimes acts as a competitor to Amazon. The real value for Amazon in the acquisition has been learning from Zappos about how to build a culture of superior customer service.

In rare instances, an acquisition comes along where 1+1 = 3 and the acquisition opens up an opportunity for the leadership team to take the best elements from both organizations to create a new entity whose combined power becomes a significant competitive force. The successful merger and integration of Exxon and Mobil, to form ExxonMobil, one of the largest corporations in the world, is a good example.

M&A Scenarios with Cultural Implications

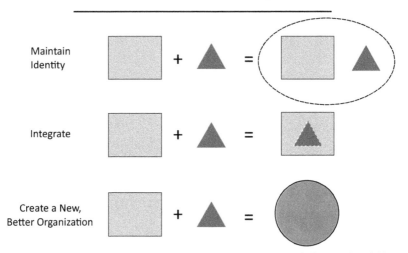

For years I have used this chart when a CEO and I are in discussions about a potential merger or acquisition. It adds the cultural dimension to the discussion and often leads to fruitful and otherwise overlooked insights.

Much like the specific processes for evaluating the strategic and cost synergies of a merger or acquisition, there can be useful processes for determining cultural similarities and differences and ways of factoring them into the overall integration plan.[78] A useful approach is:

Step 1:   Decide that culture integration will be a part of the overall M&A process and assign a specific team to it. Select members from all levels of both organizations.

Step 2: Use the business vision and strategic synergies driving the acquisition or merger to develop a picture of the intended culture that includes specific work-related behaviors and policies. Clearly define how the company will look and behave post acquisition when it is working well and creating added value. This is the *"target culture"*.

Step 3: Define the added business value you expect from the integration and define specific KPIs to measure this value creation.

Step 4: Assess the cultural strengths and weaknesses of both organizations, making certain to survey all levels and not just the senior team. Use a customized culture survey that will give you a good comparison between the two companies on the cultural items that matter.

Step 5: In a meeting with both management teams, review the survey data to determine where the cultures are most similar and different and discuss the insights and implications for making the merger work.

Step 6: Create a culture shaping plan with step-by-step milestones and KPIs. Remember to take into account all the various culture drivers.

Step 7: Engage all employees in the culture shaping plan through active communications, regular town hall meetings, and speak-up sessions to make culture a part of every staff meeting at all levels. Actively communicate examples where value is being created as a result of the integration of the two companies.

Ideally, you would start planning as soon as you decide to buy something. If you have no plan for the target company, you are going to pay the wrong price and you are not going to be ready to handle the integration. I would do a couple of days planning right at the start. At latest, I would start building a full integration plan around 100 days before you believe the deal will take place. ~Danny A. Davis

Delivering a Sustainable Turnaround

> ❝❝ *When you're in a turnaround situation, you cannot incrementalize your way out of it.* ~Steve Easterbrook

Many years ago, I led a consulting team to support the turnaround of the Ford automotive plant at Halewood, England. The Halewood Plant was by far the worst performing plant among all Ford plants globally. Not only was the quality and productivity at Halewood the worst in the company, but the union-management relationship was legendary for its militancy, with frequent strikes and work slow-downs. The plant was dirty, with cigarette butts everywhere and mattresses in several corners where supervisors would sleep during their shifts.

After decades of poor quality and high costs, Ford faced a choice of either closing the plant and devastating employment in the area, or transforming the plant into a high quality production facility for its new acquisition, Jaguar, with government funding and retaining the same employees. Everyone scoffed at the idea that those militant employees would be making high quality Jaguars instead of run of the mill Ford Escorts, which were laughingly called *"Fix Or Repair Daily"* (FORD). But Ford stepped up to a total business turnaround that involved a culture transformation as well.

After meeting with the new senior leadership team assigned to retool the plant and improve overall performance, it became obvious that the key driver of poor quality and militant union relationships was both management and a disenfranchised Union workforce. For decades the Halewood plant was considered the *"last stop on the bus"* for failed Ford managers, making it a parking lot for poor attitudes. Managers at Halewood didn't want to be there and they interacted with employees and the union in a like manner. Trust in Ford leadership and pride in the plant was non-existent. It was a toxic culture driven in large part by the collective attitudes and behaviors of disenfranchised middle managers and angry Union leaders.

 Decline causes managers to dislike and avoid one another, hide information, and deny responsibility.
~Rossabeth Moss Kanter [79]

Culture and a Sustainable Turnaround

To better understand the culture drivers responsible for this failed corporate culture system, we met and listened to numerous employees, managers and union representatives from every department. A similar story started appearing. Managers kept saying the union was blocking productivity and quality while employees and union leadership talked about how poorly they were treated, with very little communication or shared problem solving discussions. The Halewood culture was a significant business risk, and the key drivers were disenfranchised middle management and poor working conditions, exacerbated by a militant union that took advantage of the situation. And no one took accountability for poor performance.

With significant funding from both Ford and the UK government, the plant was totally retooled and the high-quality Ford Production System (based on the effective Toyota Production System) was implemented, along with extensive training for everyone from the GM all the way to the night shift, including administrative staff and secretaries.

In order to *"reset"* Halewood to accommodate a new culture, many of the former middle managers were given early retirement and a new middle manager hiring profile instituted. Halewood had a vision of being not only the highest quality plant in Ford globally but also the Ford global training center for Quality and FPS. A team of excited, optimistic, motivated and enthusiastic middle managers were required to achieve these ambitious goals. They were recruited from all over Ford globally, and had to pass rigorous interviews.

In addition, highly interactive workshops were designed and conducted for all senior executives and middle management on how to lead, coach and how to support the emerging *"New Halewood"* culture. Several Union supervisors, along with middle managers, were trained to become Culture Workshop Facilitators, who then jointly (one Middle Manager alongside one Union Supervisor) conducted culture workshops for all employees. In these workshops honest and open dialogue about the past and the future was the focus. Building renewed trust and pride in the plant were the objectives.

The only real guarantee for a sustainable turnaround is a change in culture, and the transformation at Halewood was seismic. Halewood not only produced high-quality Jaguar X-types, but also became known as the plant where upwardly-mobile managers went for training, visibility and career enhancement within Ford. Without an understanding of the real causal factors of the plant's decline and poor record, and without a concerted effort by all stakeholders to sustain the subsequent shift in the plant's culture, the massive investment in tooling, equipment and training at Halewood would have been wasted on, at best, a short-term spike in productivity.

Culture: The Turnaround Foundation

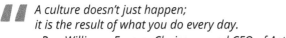 *A culture doesn't just happen;*
it is the result of what you do every day.
~Ron Williams, Former Chairman and CEO of Aetna Inc.

The turnaround of Aetna Insurance between 2000 and 2005 provides an excellent example of successfully aligning a turnaround strategy with the legacy culture and then evolving both together. In 1996, Aetna merged with U.S. Healthcare, a lower-cost health care provider. One result of this merger was a major culture clash that found the "we take care of people for life" Aetna culture resisting a more aggressive business strategy designed to take advantage of the increasingly competitive landscape of healthcare in the US.

In late 2000, John W. Rowe took over as Aetna's fourth CEO in five years. Instead of introducing another new strategy for growth, Rowe decided to leverage the historical Aetna culture of pride, quality of service to physicians, care for patients, and professionalism as the drivers of a more competitive strategy. Rather than arguing that the old culture was wrong, Rowe used the emotional attachment to the legacy culture of Aetna as a foundation for rebuilding company performance.

In 1999, Aetna was losing $1 million per day. By 2005 Aetna was earning close to $5 million a day and operating income recovered from a $300 million loss to a $1.7 billion gain, bringing the stock price from $5.84 to $48.40 a share. Rowe's insistence on a sustainable culture shift led to Aetna's current position as a leader in the healthcare insurance industry.

One of the most overlooked culture drivers for reshaping employee behavior and powering a turnaround is incentive plans. Many try to leave incentives and compensation alone for fear of demotivating the very leaders needed to deliver the turnaround. The problem is that most incentive plans are developed to focus on growth and important long-term issues like safety, employee development and operational efficiency. In a turnaround situation, the focus is on short-term survival and incentives and compensation should reflect that.

 In every company there is buried treasure: human treasure.

In most organizations there are individuals who have either deep institutional and product knowledge, or customer knowledge. In most organizations they were invisible. Yet during a turnaround these individuals can become indispensable. Many organizations have talented employees with leadership skills two or three levels down who have been overlooked or side-lined by the former leadership team. These leaders are trusted and respected by a large number of employees and are often eager to support the turnaround if given a seat at the table.

 I've been through multiple crises where the people who added the most value and impact weren't the ones sitting around the table at the beginning. I have often found great leaders two and three levels down who are just waiting for an opportunity ~Doug Yakola, McKinsey & Co.[80]

One of the biggest problems inherent in many company turnarounds is sustainability. Most professional turnaround experts are highly skilled at regaining financial stability and fixing broken operational issues. Great turnaround experts are quick to make the hard decisions that the former management team avoided. Going from negative to positive cash flow requires stopping unnecessary spending, reducing overhead costs, securing liquidity, renegotiating supply chains and wooing back lost customers. The next important step is to replace poorly-performing executives and managers. Once the company has stabilized and started on its road to recovery, the search for a new CEO begins so the interim CEO can exit. A turnaround takes a lot of work and in many cases all this work is done quickly so the owners, whether a family or private equity investors, can recoup their original investment.

Yet a few years after a successful financial turnaround, many *"saved"* companies find themselves limping along or finally going under. This is because while the financials were fixed, the culture was not. The best turnaround experts know that culture has a significant impact on success and sustainability. If the same culture drivers that caused a company to falter remain in place, there is a strong likelihood it will wind up in trouble again.

Several years ago, I attended a panel discussion at London Business School hosted by the UK Turnaround Management Association. On the panel were experts from the various professions brought in to deal with distressed companies – legal, operational, financial, advisory, banking and the CRO (Chief Restructuring Officer). I learned a lot from these turnaround professionals, but there was one key ingredient missing in all their presentations and discussions: management and employees.

Every business turnaround I have worked on always began early on with a senior leadership teambuilding lasting 3-4 days in which we not only looked at the corporate culture system and its strengths and weaknesses, but also the leadership team's strengths and weaknesses. Since organizations are shadows of their leaders, any turnaround situation should require members of the leadership team to take a long, hard look in the mirror.

 To change the outcome, change the leaders or change the leaders!

When I asked a question of the panel, *"How do you evaluate the management team when you are brought in to execute a turnaround?"* the reply I got was very similar from all the panelists. It went something like this: *"If you've been in this business long enough you develop a nose for good talent, and bad talent".*

Doesn't it seem odd that business professionals have numerous sophisticated analytical risk models and various spreadsheet templates for evaluating cash flows, return on capital, debt and risk models, sales projections, company value formulas, and sophisticated measures like EBITDA, EVA, and weighted cost of capital, but when it comes to evaluating the management team we have to resort to *"the nose"*?

Yes, it is more difficult to accurately evaluate people and teams than to evaluate risk ratios and cash flows, and maybe we shouldn't really try. What I mean is maybe the solution to a successful, sustainable business is not just about how good or bad the individual managers may be, but what the entire corporate culture system is like.

 If you can't codify what you are doing as a business process, you don't know what you're doing.
~W. Edwards Deming

What if the poor behavior and dismal business results of the management team was in large part a result of poor business processes and other culture drivers? What if improving certain culture drivers, such as meetings, product planning, budgeting, hiring, induction, promotions, performance reviews and team building, helped the management team be more effective? Work policies and processes are strong culture drivers and influence how people behave and make decisions. A common cause of poor performance in any company often lies in the business processes and culture drivers, as well as the leaders.

Some of you are now probably saying: *"But isn't it the job of executives to develop and implement effective business and management processes?"* Yes, and here lies the problem: most executives don't understand about culture drivers or the corporate culture system, and how various culture drivers interact to drive behavior and impact business performance.

I am convinced one of the reasons for the stunning turnaround at Ford Motor Company during the global financial crisis is because of the world-class business and management processes Alan Mulally brought from Boeing, replacing the old Ford culture drivers of micro-management, functional silos and excessive cost controls. Mulally left many of the same leaders in place and elevated others from within Ford, but their individual and collective behavior changed as a result of a new set of business processes and reshaped culture drivers, all of which helped reshape the Ford culture and deliver a dramatic turnaround.

The most important thing we do is to size our company, our capacity, to the correct demand and on top of that to continue to invest in the products and services, the cars and trucks, that the customers really, really want. ~Alan Mulally

Corporate Culture and Leadership Development

 Leadership and learning are indispensable from each other.
~John F. Kennedy

If there is any truth in the principle that organizations are shadows of their leaders, then the relationship between culture and leadership development becomes a critical issue for company performance and sustainability. However, most internal company leadership development programs are ineffective at producing leaders. Most are educational and interesting at best, but very few actually result in improved leadership behaviors and actions in the workplace. In many companies, attendance is required in order to be considered for a next level position. To many executives, such training is a waste of time and money.

External leadership development courses are not much better, mostly because they are generic and don't take into consideration the business context and culture of the participant's company. Many executives coming back from external leadership development training programs see the real value as networking with fellow executives from around the world, and not the development of leadership skills. For many, these programs are great for planning their next career move, but not much value for the sponsoring company.

One of the key problems with external leadership development programs is that while some good insights and skills might be gained, participants return to the same culture they left. The culture didn't attend the training, and returning participants quickly find that new leadership ideas and behaviors are not respected or well understood. External programs are more about education than leadership development.

 My main job was developing talent. I was a gardener providing water and other nourishment to our top 750 people. Of course, I had to pull out some weeds, too. ~Jack Welch

A Culture of Leadership

For decades, General Electric has been known for developing leaders who were subsequently tagged by Boards and executive recruiters to run large companies. Many GE executives went on to leadership roles in large companies, such as Home Depot, Albertsons and 3M. Larry Bossidy joined General Electric in 1957 in their financial training program and over the next 34 years took on increasing levels of leadership responsibility, including the COO of GE Credit and Vice Chairman of GE Corp. He was then recruited as CEO of industrial giant Allied-Signal and later became Chairman of Honeywell following the merger. Bossidy credits the training and development while at GE as the foundation for his business success. In 2002 he co-authored the popular business book, *Execution: The Discipline of Getting Things Done.*[81] A testament to his learning while at GE.

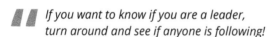 *If you want to know if you are a leader, turn around and see if anyone is following!*

GE's internal leadership development process began in 1910 and today is a 5-year application only course, and of the 200 who enter the program each year, only 2% make it to the C-Suite level within GE.[82] The program is short on classroom training and long on field experience. The official name of the program is Corporate Audit Staff, an unlikely sounding name for a leadership development program. Participants, however, have nicknamed it the Green Beret program for its rigor and high drop-out rate.

Much of the GE internal leadership development process consists of a series of 4-month projects and assignments in various GE businesses around the world working alongside established senior executives, during which upcoming leaders receive continuous feedback and honest critiques. Putting people outside their comfort zone quickly weeds out those without a hunger for new ideas and learning. Likewise, classroom training revolves around current case studies of situations within GE companies, and follows the *"GE Playbook"*, which mandates taking decisive actions, slashing costs dispassionately, streamlining operations, bolstering product development efforts, imposing financial discipline, developing teams and instituting some form of continuous process improvement such as Six Sigma training. Internal leadership development began at GE long before Jack Welch became CEO and is the outcome of a strong corporate culture where discipline, process innovation, facts and people are seen as the cornerstones for business growth and sustainability.

Why don't more companies develop strong internal leadership development programs? In a corporate culture system dominated by the drivers of cost control, functional budgets and beliefs about the importance of products and technology over people as the real business drivers, leadership development is rarely a high priority. In these cultures, senior leaders are routinely hired from the outside and tend to be paid more, inflating costs and disenfranchising ambitious internal leaders.[83]

 The growth and development of people is the highest calling of leadership. ~Harvey S. Firestone

When culture and leadership development clash, culture always wins. A recent study by James Pierce examined the US Army's professional development practice and policies for its senior-level officer corps and found that that the ability of the Army to develop future leaders in a manner that perpetuates readiness to cope with future operational and battlefield uncertainty is hampered by the Army's organizational culture [84].

Modern warfare is now more situational and context driven than at any time in history. Today's Army officers strongly believe they must operate effectively in rapidly changing situations where context matters more than pre-developed plans. However, the culture of the Army is characterized by an overarching desire for stability and control, formal rules and policies, coordination and efficiency, and hard-driving competitiveness. As a result of this incongruence between culture and leadership development, many junior officers wind up mistrusting senior management, or leaving the Army altogether.

*Effective leadership has more to do with character
and courage than IQ or business degrees.*

Another culture driver, selective hiring, plays a large part in effective leadership development. Hiring well at the entry level is a critical first step in leadership development. Many highly effective business and social leaders never attended a leadership course. Leaders who changed things for the better, like Martin Luther King, Gandhi, Mother Teresa, Andrew Carnegie, Nelson Mandela, Richard Branson, Bill Gates, Steve Jobs and even Ralph Nader made an impact through their character and courage, not their college degrees or leadership course diplomas.

Those possessing the attributes of character and courage tend to be self-starters and insatiable learners and respond well to internal development opportunities. They are driven to make a difference, not a high salary. Employees at all levels who possess character and courage have a greater tendency to step up and step in to ameliorate the effects of negative internal politics, toxic behaviors, business waste and unsustainable business practices. They see *"coachable moments"* as their responsibility to the company.

 *The purpose of leadership is to produce more leaders,
not more followers. ~Ralph Nader*

Culture and Values

 *It's not hard to make good business decisions
when you know what your values are. ~Roy Disney*

I often open my keynote talks with a question about the importance of corporate values. I ask the audience to raise their hands if they believe it is important for a company to have written values. All hands shoot up. Next, I ask how many in the audience work for a company with written values. Almost all the hands go up again. Finally, I ask them to take out a pen and paper and write down their company values. Most audiences respond with nervous laughter and sheepish looks from side to side. When I urge them to write down all their company's declared values, it only takes a few minutes before activity stops.

Over the past 35 plus years of asking this question to thousands of executives in a conference hall, or to a management team in a workshop, only about 40% can accurately name all their stated company values. One study suggests that for front-line employees, where the values are supposed to be an even stronger guide to work behavior and decision making, only 23% of U.S. employees strongly agree they can apply their organization's values to their work every day, and only 27% believe in their organization's values.[85]

 Written values statements are not the corporate culture.

An aligned culture enables execution, decision making and positively impacts business results. Culture, in such companies, becomes a competitive advantage and even helps attract and retain top talent. Values should convey what makes a company successful, and processes should have the corporate values deliberately woven into them. However, written values that few can remember and are just PR slogans weaken the organization's overall confidence, integrity, and ability to compete. In this case, written values become a performance liability.

Weaving Values into the Culture

Tony Hsieh, CEO of Zappos.com has long been a champion of building companies with strong values, and he believes that values must be deeply woven into the corporate culture system in order to help produce sustainable business results.

 Values are not the culture, but can be one of the important drivers that form and sustain employee behavior. If they are 'real'. And one of the really interesting things I found is that it actually doesn't matter what your values are, what matters is that you have them and that you align the organization around them. And the power actually comes from the alignment, not from the actual values.
~Tony Hsieh

Enron is a classic example of meaningless, or better yet, systematically ignored corporate values. The stated Enron values of Integrity, Communication, Respect, Excellence were prominently displayed in the lobby and even chiseled into the marble of their Houston headquarters office. Behind these four words was the Enron Code of Ethics Manual, a 64-page handbook that not only outlined the company's mission and core values, but also the various ethical policies that all employees were expected to follow. Yet the CEO and senior leaders routinely made decisions that proved to be highly unethical, fraudulent and criminal. And in the case of several decisions made by the CFO, the Board voted to suspend the ethics code so such decisions could go ahead. The profit potential was too high, and the greed even higher. Needless to say this behavior filtered down into the organization, especially within Enron Trading.

Corporate values are far from useless, and they are not a thing of the past. For values to be meaningful, it is critical they are integrated into daily business activities, and also embedded in company policies and processes. Values that are never openly discussed have very little impact.

The Johnson & Johnson Company, founded in 1886, is now a global medical devices, pharmaceutical and health products company with 127,000 employees and revenues of $71 billion. Its success has often been attributed to the *J&J Credo*, a set of values and responsibilities set down by Robert Wood Johnson II, son of the founder, in 1943. The Credo puts the company's responsibilities in the following order: patients, doctors and nurses first, employees second, communities third and shareholders last.[86] The *J&J Credo* is unique for the way it turns values and responsibilities into actionable behaviors:

 Johnson & Johnson Credo

> *We believe our first responsibility is to the doctors, nurses and patients, to mothers and fathers and all others who use our products and services. In meeting their needs everything we do must be of high quality. We must constantly strive to reduce our costs in order to maintain reasonable prices. Customers' orders must be serviced promptly and accurately. Our suppliers and distributors must have an opportunity to make a fair profit.*

> *We are responsible to our employees, the men and women who work with us throughout the world. Everyone must be considered as an individual. We must respect their dignity and recognize their merit. They must have a sense of security in their jobs. Compensation must be fair and adequate, and working conditions clean, orderly and safe. We must be mindful of ways to help our employees fulfill their family responsibilities. Employees must feel free to make suggestions and complaints. There must be equal opportunity for employment, development and advancement for those qualified. We must provide competent management, and their actions must be just and ethical.*

> *We are responsible to the communities in which we live and work and to the world community as well. We must be good citizens – support good works and charities and bear our fair share of taxes. We must encourage civic improvements and better health and education. We must maintain in good order the property we are privileged to use, protecting the environment and natural resources.*

> *Our final responsibility is to our stockholders. Business must*

make a sound profit. We must experiment with new ideas. Research must be carried on, innovative programs developed and mistakes paid for. New equipment must be purchased, new facilities provided and new products launched. Reserves must be created to provide for adverse times. When we operate according to these principles, the stockholders should realize a fair return.

At Johnson & Johnson, the *Credo* is used as a lens for evaluating strategic and business decisions. Because the *Credo* is such a central aspect of corporate decision-making, it is actively debated on a regular basis by executives and managers to make certain they remain current, relevant and well understood. The *J&J Credo* is also central to their employee on-boarding program, where its content is embedded throughout with a wide variety of examples and case studies.

One of the best ways to ensure Values become a business asset and not just words on paper or historical artifacts, is to link them to compensation and promotion criteria. According to former McKinsey & Co. managing director Ian Davis, *"the values of a company, to be meaningful, must be reflected in the key managerial processes, such as performance evaluation and appointments. A company's values are judged by actions and behavior, not words and mission statements".*[87]

A critical step in this integration of values into the culture is to translate the corporate values into a series of non-negotiable behaviors that are directly linked to the business strategy. In other words, it should be crystal clear how values support effective strategy execution. Unless explicitly spelled out as work behaviors, values are subject to multiple interpretations, especially in a global company where different national cultures work together. Employees from different national cultures can interpret the same value very differently, which can lead to fragmentation or misalignment within the organization.

Suppose a global company has significant operations in multiple countries, such as Australia, Russia, Japan, Pakistan, Turkey, China and India, and one of their core values is Openness. Imagine how these different cultures could interpret that word. In Japan, the value of *'openness'* is easily interpreted as openly agreeing with the boss. In Australia, the value of *'openness'* means back-and-forth discussions raising multiple points of view, and often with a great deal of energy and colorful language. In Russia, the value of 'openness' is treated with the suspicion of personal agendas and internal politics. In India, the value of *'openness'* is often interpreted as entrepreneurship and the ability to do what one wants, even inside the company. So much for an aligned corporate culture and behaviors.

Even without the complication of national cultures, a stated corporate value without clearly defined behaviors attached to it can cause confusion within the same company location. In a company where one of the most important values is Innovation, an employee working in the marketing department and an employee working in the finance department trying to be innovative could easily have different interpretations and behaviors. Thus values-based behaviors should be articulated in such a way as to be appropriate for the specifics of each different department and team. You cannot expect a software developer to be rated under the same exact behavior for the value of Accountability as a customer service representative when their daily tasks are completely different.

Another way to bring Values to life is to embed them in performance reviews and promotion criteria, as well as factors that go into determining bonuses and compensation. To support the turnaround of Aetna, specific behaviors relating to company values made up a large percentage of executive performance evaluations and compensation.

 Don't lower your expectations to meet your performance.
Raise your level of performance to meet your expectations.
~Ralph Marston

Culture and the Customer

> *The battle for business success has always been around the customer experience. The business world is only now realizing it.*

Most company strategy and operations meetings are packed, standing room only, mainly because everyone wants to represent their function, protect their departmental budgets, and push their ideas for new projects or more funding. The room is full of people, ideas, and agendas, some open and obvious, several hidden.

It's not far off to say that most company meeting time is taken up with internal issues. Costs, budgets, schedules and sales usually lead the way and it is this type of inside-out thinking and behavior that tends to create more problems than it actually solves.[88] Many years ago I supported a very talented new General Manager, Ian Walsh, turn around a nearly bankrupt, once market leading aircraft engine company, Lycoming Engines. One of the key issues Ian and his leadership team focused on was, Voice of the Customer. In fact, their vision was written as: *"Return to Profitability by Listening to the Voice of Our Customers"*. And they did both.

Who pays your salary?

If you say the company, you have failed Business 101A! The customer pays your salary! Without customers buying your products and services, and telling their friends and social networks to shop at your stores or use your services, your business will stagnate. Research by American Express shows that customers are willing to pay on average 14% more for excellent customer service. In addition to spending more, people who receive good customer service tell an average of eight people about their good experience and word of mouth is highly effective in bringing in new customers. Forty-two percent of Americans surveyed said that a recommendation from a friend or family member will get them to do business with a new company, even more than a sale or promotion (34%) or a company's reputation or brand (15%).[89]

 A corporate culture system designed around the customer has a high probability of delivering and sustaining business success.

I often assess a senior leadership team on their focus and alignment around certain key business issues. No matter what the industry, issues relating to customer experience, customer data, customer satisfaction, customer wants and needs tend to score the lowest. More leadership teams are focused on internal operations, budgets, costs and schedules than on the customer.

Despite the large amount spent by most consumer companies on customer service training and product advertising, customers are not experiencing greatly improved service levels. In the latest American Express Global Customer Service survey, only 5% of those surveyed said companies are currently exceeding their customer service expectations. In addition, 38% said that they believe companies are paying less attention to providing good customer service.[89] External customers have choice and they vote with their feet and their wallet.

Why have customers seen a decline in service levels recently? One big answer is the shift to technology platforms and outsourcing for customer interactions. To save costs, many companies have turned to technologies like automated phone response systems, online service inquiries and internet portals. Another reason for declines in customer service is the belief by many companies that as a company grows larger it needs more rules, targets and objectives to control staff behaviors. A culture of excessive rules and controls tends to blunt staff initiative and reduce the use of discretion in customer interactions. A good example is the recent United Airlines fiasco of physically ejecting a paying customer in order to make room for its own staff. This is obviously a case where a culture of rules trumped a culture of common sense and courtesy.

 Customer service shouldn't just be a department,
It should be the entire company. ~Tony Hsieh

Serving the Customer is the Culture

Nordstrom Department Stores continue to deliver exceptional customer service and post positive financial performance in a difficult retail environment with a simple one-line customer service policy: Use Common Sense. Nordstrom backs this up with strong culture drivers, such as in-depth staff on-boarding and training, selective hiring, compensation and sales commissions based on service, and numerous hero stories about the type of customer service expected. Nordstrom staff training is filled with specific, observable behaviors, such as:[90]

- o Don't point. If a customer has a question about where something is located, walk them there.
- o After ringing up the sale, always walk the bagged purchase around the counter and hand it to the customer, never hand it across the counter.
- o Offer to ring up a customer's purchase so they don't have to stand in line.
- o Answer the phone by the second ring.

A service culture made real! Nordstrom provides an excellent example of a corporate-culture-system that reinforces good customer service behaviors, and their positive financial performance is a sign of the dividends of using common sense and multiple culture drivers to create great service and customer loyalty.

 If there's one reason we have done better than of our peers
in the Internet space over the last six years, it is because we
have focused like a laser on customer experience, and that
really does matter, I think, in any business. It certainly matters
online, where word of mouth is so very, very powerful.
~Jeff Bezos

Culture and Internal Customers

And what about internal customers? Most companies pay little attention to service levels for internal customers, yet this is another case where culture has a dramatic impact on overall business performance. Very few companies have cultural guidelines, training and specific behaviors for internal customer service between functions, even though poor handoffs and delayed sharing of information between functions or departments can dramatically impact business performance and financial results. To deliver effective internal customer service, all departments must work together on shared objectives, agree on effective, cross-functional processes and procedures, and align around service expectations. In most companies these internal culture drivers are missing from the corporate-culture-system.

Consider the relationship between product engineering and sales support. The sales support function is responsible for taking orders from customers and solving problems for what are often highly technical in nature. Sales reps often need clarification from an engineer to process a customer order for the correct part, but engineers view information requests from the Sales Support department as low priority, uninteresting, and annoying. After all, their goals are based on new product designs, efficiency and cost reductions. Mutual annoyance between departments is a normal and frustrating situation within many organizations, but to the external customer, delays in the delivery of parts and service is more than an annoyance. And to a commercial customer it can mean reduced profits and reputation damage.

Inside every modern organization there are literally hundreds of cross-functional requests that can have a negative impact on company revenue because frustrated external customers will look for other solutions. In one organization, the calculated cost to the company of one incorrect shipment was approximately $125,000 in wasted labor, materials, and other expenses. In addition, the cost of frustration and delayed deadlines to the external customer was damaging to the company's brand and reputation, and future sales.[91]

Does your company have a culture of excellent internal customer service? Are there specific cross-functional shared objectives? Is the compensation of function heads based on internal customer feedback and service levels? How often do different departments get together to understand how they each impact the other and ultimately, the external customer?

Culture and the Call Center

One place where corporate culture interfaces directly with customers on a 24/7 basis is the Call Center, and most callers hang up being more frustrated than satisfied. The growth of local and offshore Call Centers has been explosive over the past two decades as companies seek ways to reduce overall costs. But the move to Call Centers has in many cases had a negative impact on customer satisfaction and loyalty. The corporate culture system within a call center is the major culprit.

Tony Hsieh, CEO of Zappos.com has a particular view of call centers, not as a cost saving opportunity, but as another opportunity to WOW! customers. As of December 2012, Zappos's longest call was 10 hours and 29 minutes, and it is celebrated as an example of taking responsibility to solve a tough problem and super-satisfy the customer. Traditional call centers use a metric called average-handle-time to gauge efficiency and staff productivity, and the lower the better. Hsieh says Zappos is more focused on creating great customer service than call time efficiency.

 I think the main thing is just trust [the customer service reps] and let them make their own decisions. Most call centers are set up by policies and so the actual person that's answering the phone doesn't really have the ability to do anything. If you... call most customer service places, if you ask for anything that's not normal they have to talk to a supervisor or just say 'oh our policy doesn't allow that' and whatever. So we generally try to stay away from policies, we just ask our reps to do whatever they feel is the right thing to do for the customer and the company. And that's actually really uncomfortable for a lot of reps that come from other call centers. We kind of have to untrain their bad habits.[92]

If customer service is one of the best indicators of company performance, what culture drivers need to be in place? A culture of customer service rests on four strong culture drivers:

- o   Investment in people
- o   Technology supporting frontline workers
- o   Recruiting and training practices
- o   Compensation linked to performance

Working together, these four drivers produce the behaviors that delight customers and resolve issues quickly. By delighting customers, an organization will create customer loyalty, generating repeat business and strong word-of-mouth recommendations.[93]

Okay, a service culture sounds like a good goal, but how much to invest in all these service-culture drivers? And what's the return on this investment? Will it be profitable, or just a nice experience for customers?

The reason many companies don't invest in superior customer service is that they can't answer these questions with real data. Bain & Company has conducted several studies to help quantify the ROI on building a service culture.[94] A place to start is to research your most loyal, repeat customers and evaluate the margins generated from frequency of shopping, spend per visit, annual spend, average cost of customer complaints, number of referrals. You can even factor in the cost of sales to a new customer versus an existing customer, which in one study was shown to be 113% higher.[95] And repeat customers have fewer bad debts.

Reichheld and Sasser estimate that a 5% increase in customer loyalty can produce profit increases from 25% to 85% and conclude that customer loyalty is a better indicator of company performance than market share.[96]

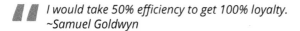 *I would take 50% efficiency to get 100% loyalty.*
~Samuel Goldwyn

Culture and Middle Management

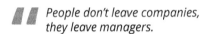 *People don't leave companies,*
they leave managers.

The attitudes and actions of middle management, how they behave in the workplace and in daily interactions with employees, have a much larger influence on employee behavior, productivity and morale, and the overall culture than most people realize. Yet in culture study after study middle management is virtually ignored; the focus being on either the senior leadership and employees.

People don't leave companies. They leave managers. The attitudes and behavior of middle management is a powerful culture driver. The role of leadership is to set direction, develop strategy, determine ways to beat the competition, and establish internal ground rules, values, and operating principles. Front-line employees put these into practice. The front-line is where the work gets done and where the customer meets the company. However, the vision, values, ground rules and objectives are rarely given to front-line employees by the CEO or the senior leadership team: they are interpreted and often filtered by middle management.

A major role of middle management is to translate strategy, policies and business objectives into work-place ground rules and behaviors, and sometimes these translations get confused or misrepresented. Since middle managers are often left out of senior meetings where issues are discussed and decisions made, they often do the best they can to translate accurately. However, many middle managers also feel disenfranchised, especially in a culture where many of the upper management positions are filled from the outside and there are few opportunities for personal development or advancement.

 I've been promoted to middle management.
I never thought I'd sink so low. ~Tim Gould

Middle Management Culture

Middle management is an important part of the company performance equation, and the corporate culture system, yet most companies focus more attention, development time and money on senior management and front-line employees than on middle managers. Middle managers have a great deal of real influence on a company's culture and the day-to-day life of employees, including how work is done and beliefs about leadership and the company.

This simple graphic analogy shows the important role of middle management in determining the culture at the front line. And it is at the front line that most customers experience the culture of the company. Customers don't sit in the Executive Conference Room, but they do sit in the waiting room at the hospital or stand in line at the check-out counter, or try to get a problem resolved from the Call Center. It is easy to see how a culture can get out of alignment with the vision, values and strategy. In some instances, middle management can act as a barrier to execution, innovation and change.

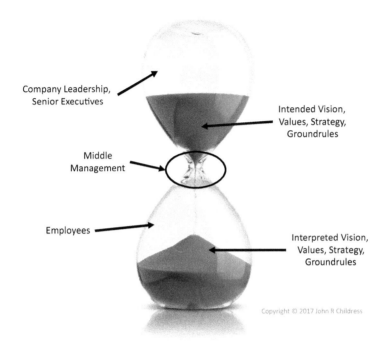

Company Leadership, Senior Executives

Intended Vision, Values, Strategy, Groundrules

Middle Management

Employees

Interpreted Vision, Values, Strategy, Groundrules

Copyright © 2017 John R Childress

> **❚❚** *While organizations may be shadows of their leaders, culture at the employee level is often a shadow of middle management!*

In engineering and technology companies, the value of management is often questioned. After all, technical excellence is what earns most people praise and respect from their peers and coworkers. At best, engineers see management as a distraction, and at worst, an impediment to *"real work"*.

Google is a good example. [97] At one point the founders, Larry Page and Sergey Brin wondered if managers were really necessary in a fast moving technology company. In 2002 they adopted a flat organization structure, eliminating all engineering management positions in an attempt to create more open communication, collegiality and rapid development. It was a failure because many people started coming directly to them with questions about expense reports, interpersonal conflicts, and other management issues.

Middle Management Matters

With this experiment, it wasn't long before Page and Brin realized that managers contributed in important ways. For instance, by communicating strategy, helping employees prioritize projects, facilitating collaboration, supporting career development, and ensuring that processes and systems align with company goals.

To avoid micromanaging and encourage individual initiative, it is not uncommon for a manager at Google to have 30 direct reports. And the company uses a data-driven hiring process to find young, ambitious self-starters and original thinkers as a strong driver of the culture. But as Google has grown, many of these self-starters began to rebel at being promoted to management positions. Google used its own internal data to prove the value of management to individual and team performance.

Google launched Project Oxygen, a multi-year internal research initiative, to investigate how much management matters. After gathering and analyzing data on 10,000 performance reviews, surveys, and nominations for top-manager awards, Google's internal research found that employees with high-scoring bosses consistently reported greater satisfaction in innovation, work-life balance, and career development. Also, high quality managers showed less staff turnover.

Google came to the realization that their cultural bias of promoting managers based on technical excellence was totally flawed. *"It turns out that's absolutely the least important thing"*, reports Laslo Brock, former Google head of HR. *"It's important, but pales in comparison. Much more important is just making that connection and being accessible"*.[98]

Great managers consistently exhibit particular behaviors, and demonstrations of technical excellence are among the least important. Google's internal data points to 8 key eight habits highly associated with effective management:

1. Be a good coach;
2. Empower your team and don't micromanage;
3. Express interest in employee's success and well-being;
4. Be productive and results-oriented;
5. Be a good communicator and listen to your team;
6. Help employees with career development;
7. Have a clear vision and strategy for the team;

8. Have key technical skills, so you can help advise the team.

When was the last time your company spent as much time and development dollars on middle management as they do on senior executives and front-line employees? Are middle managers in your company trained on any of the eight essential management behaviors noted above? When was the last time middle managers were invited to sit in on senior management strategy meetings? When was the last time middle managers were asked to speak at company meetings, or Board Meetings, or industry conferences?

 At one point in their lives, all great leaders were rookies and middle managers.

Culture and Employee Engagement

▌▌ Give a man a fish and you will feed him for a day. Teach him to fish and he will feed himself and others for a lifetime.

Corporate culture and employee engagement have recently surfaced in numerous global surveys as a critical business issue. In a 2015 Deloitte study, 87 percent of organizations rate culture and engagement as their top challenges, and 50 percent call the problem *"very important"*. [99] According to the Gallup polling firm, only 13 percent of the global workforce is *"highly engaged"*.[100] Upwards of half the workforce would not recommend their employer to their peers.[101] Overall the level of employee engagement has fallen steadily in the past decade with 37% reported to be either passive or totally disengaged at work.[102] On the other hand, highly-engaged employees are correlated with business performance, strong earnings growth, innovation, change agility, and a high-performance culture.

Employee engagement and culture are now real business issues, and not just a topic for HR to debate. Employee engagement is more than just earning a pay check and doing what is prescribed in your job description. Engagement refers to the additional and voluntary emotional, physical and mental effort a person puts into their workplace efforts. The key word here is voluntary.

Employees rating themselves as highly engaged are more than twice as likely to remain in the company as those rating themselves disengaged. Numerous studies conclude that companies with higher levels of employee engagement tend to outperform those with lower employee engagement. For example, a five-point increase in employee engagement has been linked to a three-point increase in revenue growth in the following year.[102]

Beyond a pay check, what positive benefits do we get from work? What would cause an employee to give additional, voluntary effort? Here is where love comes into the workplace. There are three types of love that act as culture drivers for high levels of employee engagement:

o **I love the work I do**. It is easy to give voluntary effort, to think about work challenges when you are not at work, and to come up with new ideas to enhance your work when work is intellectually stimulating, when you learn and grow as a person because of the work, and when you learn something new about yourself and the world.

o **I love the people I work with**. Voluntary engagement is easy when you are surrounded by people who bring out the best in you, who support and challenge you, who help and coach you, who help you improve as an employee and a person

o **I love this company.** It is easy to foster high employee engagement in an organization where managers and senior leaders work hard to remove barriers to work, reduce bureaucracy, provide tools to make work easier and faster, where ideas are listened to with respect and thoughtfulness, where there exists a higher purpose than just profit or revenue, where products and services are of high quality, where the customer is at the heart of the business, where goals are challenging instead of punitive, and where there are ample opportunities for self-development and advancement .

Why do people voluntarily give more than they are paid for? Human psychology tells us that much of our voluntary behavior is driven by either avoiding pain or gaining a positive benefit. Let's hope your work culture is more about benefit than pain.

Culture, Trust and Engagement

In his recent bestselling business book, *The Speed of Trust*,[103] management guru Stephen M. R. Covey makes an overwhelming case for trust as a key driver of a culture of strong employee engagement and superior business performance. Realizing that the word, Trust, must be translated into behaviors to be effective in shaping performance, Covey goes into great detail on 13 workplace trust behaviors that form the basis of a high-performance culture.

From the standpoint of corporate culture, employee engagement is a two-way street: leaders and managers must work to engage the employee, who in turn must choose the level of engagement to offer the employer. The accountability is on both the company and the employee. Based on their visits to 44 plants and surveys of more than 4,000 employees, Eileen Appelbaum and her colleagues concluded that companies are indeed more successful when managers share knowledge and power with workers and when workers assume increased responsibility and use discretion rather than rules to solve customer problems.[104]

 In times of global uncertainty and volatility, the conventional wisdom doesn't always apply when it comes to improving engagement. ~Aon Hewitt

With the increasing pace of globalization, growing social unrest and mistrust of political systems, fear of job loss due to technology, and increasing levels of everyday stress acting as external pressures on employee well-being, businesses must work harder to deliver a culture where employee engagement can grow and flourish. To help foster greater employee engagement, business must go beyond the traditional internal amenities like safety, training, good bosses, adequate pay and benefits, and interesting work. The focus must also be on how the company impacts society, local communities and the environment.[105]

In some instances, corporate culture acts as de facto compensation.[106] Companies that once used hefty salary packages to attract top talent no longer have the same resources as they may have pre-recession, so non-cash benefits like culture and company values become a way to attract and retain new talent.

To improve engagement and culture, CEOs need to go beyond PowerPoint presentations and all-hands meetings. The 2017 Edelman study reports the credibility of CEO's at an all-time low globally, with a trust level of just 37%.[105] Peers are more credible and trusted than leaders or upper management. This represents an opportunity for all leaders to Step Up and Step In in order to cast a longer and more positive leadership shadow.

Deliberately Developmental Cultures

A few organizations have understood that culture is really a business system with inputs, drivers and outputs. And by designing culture drivers that support the personal goals of employees is one way to improve and sustain performance, innovation and engagement. In a recent book, *An Everyone Culture: Becoming a Deliberately Developmental Organization*,[136] Harvard professors Robert Kegan, Lisa Lahey and their co-authors postulate that an organization will best perform when the internal systems, policies and processes are designed and aligned with people's strongest motive, which is to grow, as a person and as a professional. Their research focuses on three organizations that go beyond just having good people development programs, coaching and yearly off-sites. They create a corporate culture system focused on development, learning and personal and professional growth that is woven into the daily fabric of working life and the company's regular operations, daily routines, and conversations.

In the Deliberately Developmental Organization model, the purpose is to provide a place where people can grow and the entire internal business is designed to make personal and professional growth the core of the business. The benefit is that, with good hiring models and the use of modern technologies, employees will be fully engaged in their jobs because they are growing and learning at the same time.

One example is Next Jump, an e-commerce company that handles loyalty programs for companies like Dell, AARP, Intel, and Hilton Hotels. Next Jump has over 28,000 merchant partners, both retailers and manufacturers, with offices in New York City, Boston, San Francisco and London. Their Perks-at-Work e-commerce platform serves over 70 million employees around the globe generating over $2 billion in sales in 2016.

To help support its culture and purpose, Next Jump has developed numerous apps for internal use in developing and growing its employees, such as apps for feedback, peer recognition and performance reviews. And it has a 3-month new employee orientation process that is more like a leadership boot camp than a typical on-boarding program.

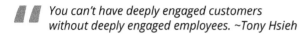 *You can't have deeply engaged customers without deeply engaged employees. ~Tony Hsieh*

A Culture for Innovation

Building a culture where people feel comfortable trying things that might fail starts with senior leaders' attitudes and role modelling.

The American Civil War (1861-1865) was one of the bloodiest wars in American history, with over 1,100,000 casualties and more than 620,000 killed. Many of those wounded ended up as amputees. After the gruesome amputation of a damaged arm or leg with crude saws and no anesthetics, the prospect of a productive livelihood was slim. At that time standard army prosthetics consisted of a wooden peg leg or a stiff crudely carved arm and hand.

James Edward Hanger was 18 years old and just three days into his role as a Confederate soldier when on June 3rd, 1861 he became the first casualty of the Civil War after a cannon ball smashed into his leg. Fitted with the standard army peg-leg after the amputation, Hanger was eventually released from a Union prison and returned home to Virginia, where he locked himself in his room for three months.

In his room Hanger began to develop the first articulated artificial limb and knee-joint. For Hanger, this new prosthetic was a requirement to get back to his productive former life as a trained engineer. It also became his future livelihood. The newly designed artificial limb quickly came into great demand from other Civil War casualties, and later from casualties during WWI. Over the next several decades, Hanger Prosthetics became a nationwide medical organization that dramatically improved the lives of thousands of amputees.[107] Today, the Hanger Group is a collection of R&D, prosthetics and rehabilitation companies that has nearly 25% of the global prosthetics market and remains a leader in prosthetics innovation.

 One person can make a difference, and everyone should try.
~John F Kennedy

And if you ever interact with one of the Hanger companies, you will hear the story of James Edward Hanger at least a thousand times. The values and the purpose that drove young Hanger to make a difference are still very much alive within the Hanger organizations. The company purpose and a culture of accountability drives employees at all levels to continuously innovate, to help people lead better lives, to make a difference, and a profit.

Foundation for an Innovation Culture

Two things are critical for the establishment of a culture of innovation. A deep dissatisfaction with the current levels of customer service or product capabilities, coupled with a strong belief that individual and collective efforts inside a company can make a difference.

 Most senior executives have a very strong sense of organizational ownership and accountability, but I think what people and companies have to own is an innovation agenda.
~Satya Nadella, CEO Microsoft

Dissatisfaction without accountability leads to complaints, but little change. With new technology disrupting every business and industry and new competitors emerging from all corners of the globe, more and more business leaders see innovation in products and services as a way to deliver competitive advantage. Sustainability certainly requires continuous innovation.

There are no fail safe best-practice solutions or organization designs that guarantee continuous innovation. There is no statistically significant relationship between financial performance and spending for innovation, in terms of total R&D dollars or R&D as a percentage of revenues.[108] Nevertheless, innovation is becoming an increasingly important aspect of every business. After studying innovation among 759 companies based in 17 major markets, researchers found that corporate culture was a much more important driver of radical innovation than labor, capital, government policies or national culture.[109]

The major culture driver of innovation is investment in people. A McKinsey study on leadership and innovation found that 94% of senior executives believe that people and corporate culture are the most important drivers of innovation.[110] Many senior executives believe their existing corporate culture makes it difficult to free up top talent for projects to meet innovation goals. While 40% of executives surveyed believe their company does not have enough talent for the innovation projects they pursue, most employees believe their organizations have the right talent, but the corporate culture drivers are too focused on costs and risk and not on customers and innovation.

Very few companies put innovation as a formal strategic objective answerable to the Board. In one global study of 1000 companies, 36% of all respondents admitted that their innovation strategy is not well aligned to their company's overall strategy, and 47% said their corporate culture does not support their innovation strategy.[110] One recognized leader in product innovation is the 3M Company, which sets a formal strategic objective of earning 30 percent of its revenues from products introduced in the past five years.

When the degree of alignment between company culture and formal innovation strategy was correlated with annual growth over a five-year period, companies with a high degree of alignment experienced 12% faster growth over five years and their gross profit grew 7% faster.[110] The major culture drives behind these increases were internal policies that supported innovation projects with adequate funding and talent. A mandate for innovation without a budget is a design to fail.

Both management and employees agree that a strong culture of innovation is characterized by a tolerance for risk, recognition for new ideas and innovative projects, coupled with management support for allocated time and funding. In companies with an innovation culture, leadership routinely involves employees from all levels in discussing new ideas and planning for innovation. A survey of 600 executives and managers indicated that trust and engagement were the culture drivers most required for a culture of innovation. Most companies however, don't have a culture that actively supports innovation and risk, and upwards of 46 percent of the professionals surveyed said they would seek out a trusted colleague or peer before going to management for feedback on their innovation projects and new ideas.[108]

Even within the same company, subcultures can be more or less innovative. In a 2006 study of four internal departments within Liberty Life Insurance Company, the data shows clearly that an innovative department delivers better performance than either a supportive or bureaucratic department culture.[111] Innovative cultures allow for greater individual discretion in accomplishing tasks and meeting deadlines. In this case, Service Level Agreements being the time allotted to deliver various components of service.

Culture and Performance, Liberty Life
(Data from Geldenhuys, 2006)

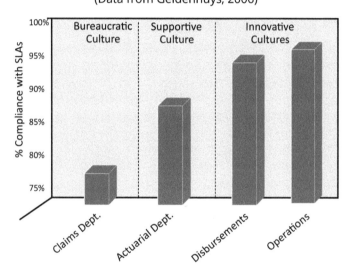

For companies looking to move towards a culture of innovation, start by seeking out those internal departments or subcultures that display the characteristics of innovation. Then determine the culture drivers at play in those departments and use them as a template for developing innovation subcultures throughout the company.

Another strong culture driver of innovation is *"voice of the customer"*. Fred Palensky, EVP of Research and Development at 3M, a recognized leader in product innovation, states the opportunity clearly:

 Our goal is to include the voice of the customer at the basic research level and throughout the product development

cycle, to enable our technical people to actually see how their technologies work in various market conditions.[108]

The *"voice of the customer"* is more than surveys and opinion polls; it is a commitment to actively engaging customers in the product development process and in evaluating current products and services.

Drivers of an Innovation Culture

Boston Consulting Group has been studying innovative companies for several years and finds that only 8% of companies in their global survey are consistent breakthrough innovators.[112] Breakthrough innovators differ significantly in several primarily organizational and cultural characteristics:

- o Innovation project approval does not depend on projected ROI
- o Flatter organization structures for innovation projects
- o Culture of openness, transparency and cross-functional collaboration
- o Policies and processes supporting risk tolerance and experimentation
- o KPIs for innovation projects based on longer time frames and heavily weighted towards customer-driven metrics

How does a large, well established organization create an innovation culture? In 2000, IBM decided to establish a new internal initiative called the Emerging Business Opportunity (EBO) department that focused on pure product innovation experiments. In essence they created multiple start-ups. Some of the initiatives failed, but seven of those original *"business experiments"* succeeded and in the first five years added $15.2 billion to IBM's top line; more than twice as much as acquisitions.[113]

Some established companies have tried adopting a 5% rule, allowing employees to devote a share of their daily work time and budget to new ideas and innovative solutions. However, in most cultures this rarely results in profitable innovations since the legacy corporate culture system built on efficiency and cost control tends to take precedence.

Asking an employee to experiment and develop new ideas while at the same time being cost efficient and getting things right the first time is akin to combining an orchestra and a jazz band and expecting to get a high quality concert. Nucor Steel, 3M and W.L. Gore are successful large companies that have a strong culture of encouraging innovation where numerous culture drivers, such as selective hiring, peer performance reviews, small teams and individual accountability allow the entrepreneurial spirit and innovation to flourish. All three are successful, large companies which routinely rank among the best companies to work for.

 For over 100 years, 3M has had a culture of interdependence, collaboration, even co-dependence. Our businesses are all interdependent and collaboratively connected to each other, across geographies, across businesses, and across industries. The key is culture.
~Fred Palensky, 3M Company

Since culture works on human logic, not business logic, trying to create a culture of innovation can go against some of our basic human characteristics, particularly those related to uncertainty, risk and peer pressure. Most of us are conditioned to continue with those behaviors and work practices that made us successful in the past. It's the basis of how people develop habits of behavior and beliefs. Humans subconsciously resist trying new things that have a high degree of uncertainty. It's our built-in, anti-failure mechanism. In the corporate environment, aversion to trying new ways of working or embracing new ideas increases as people become more specialized and rewarded for unique skills.

Subject-matter experts are often highly critical of new ideas and approaches. Employees are routinely rewarded for having the right answer and earn the respect of their peers. In many companies, recognition for quick solutions and fixes drive behavior more than exploring long-term opportunities. Risks that can be calculated are easier for people to accept than the uncertainty of innovation, which requires short-term losses for potential long-term gains.

How to overcome, or at least blunt the innate risk-aversion elements of human behavior? One proven approach is to establish dedicated, protected spaces for experimentation. In addition, a premium should be placed on the recruitment of people with the required personal traits of curiosity and risk preference. A classic example is the Skunk Works within the Lockheed Martin Corporation, which has created revolutionary aircraft and technology over the last 70 years by investing in people and building a culture of risk and innovation.

 For more than 70 years, the Skunk Works has existed to create revolutionary aircraft and technologies that push the

boundaries of what is possible. Our unique culture is the key to our success – the secret ingredient that will define the solutions for the next 70 years and beyond.
~Lockheed Martin Skunk Works

Culture and Technology

 Organizational culture is one of the main barriers to company success in the digital age. ~McKinsey & Co.

Only recently have executives started talking about technology change and culture change at the same forums and conferences. And often in the same sentence. A decade earlier, these two business elements were seen as opposites, the yin and yang of corporate life. The hard and the soft side of business. One worshiped, the other ignored. But with the rapid advancement of technology and the transformation of industry after industry by the global Internet and social media, even young start-up companies find themselves faced with the challenges of having to rethink their business model and culture drivers on a regular basis. While larger corporations can't be as nimble or take an all-or-nothing approach to the adoption of new technologies and a digital business model, every large established organization, in order to survive, will eventually embark on a business transformation program.

And here is where corporate culture comes in. According to a recent McKinsey survey, three corporate culture drivers stand out as significant barriers to business success in the digital age:

- o functional silos
- o weak customer focus

o   risk aversion.

While these three culture drivers negatively impact business performance in most organizations, they are especially acute when companies try to adopt a digital business model.[114] The same study also shows that these three culture elements have a significant correlation to negative business performance.

A recent BMC Software survey of more than 3,200 office workers in 12 countries showed on average 40% fear they won't be able to keep up with the rate of change required by digital business, while 88% placed the responsibility to create innovative cultures on their employers.[115]

 Entering the digital economy cannot wait until the culture is right.

Cultural Agility and Digital Transformation

Companies must combine their technology transformation activities with a simultaneous focus on reshaping these three critical culture drivers, among others, in order to make their organizations more responsive to customers, more willing to embrace risks and investments in technology, and better connected across functions and departments. Success with a digital business model requires the organization to deliver value to the customer through a series of horizontal, cross functional business processes which are difficult to deliver with stand-alone functions, each with their own functional objectives. Success with a digital business model requires joining the dots in end-to-end customer-centric processes enabled by technology.

To help shape a corporate culture that supports a digital business model, companies are hiring from non-traditional sources, such as start-ups and pure digital-play companies to infuse their organizations with new ways of looking at risk, technology adoption and the customer experience. Starbucks, for example, created a digital-ventures team, hiring vice presidents from Google, Microsoft, and Razorfish to drive outside thinking about risk and customer-focus.

Using technology to provide Call Center staff with real-time information on purchase history, buying preferences and other key customer information helps them improve service and resolve customer issues without having to escalate to management. And digital tools in the manufacturing environment can be used for predictive maintenance, giving authority for equipment refurbishment to front-line staff instead of management. Digital tools combined with a culture of greater risk preference ultimately can lead to faster turnaround times, greater customer satisfaction and reduced overall company costs.

When the external environment is changing rapidly, internal risk-taking and goal-setting needs to keep pace. The New York Times set a goal of doubling its digitally-derived revenues in under five years. Nordstrom has invested more than $1.4 billion in technology to improve cross-channel sales to better compete with on-line retailers like Amazon. And in banking and financial services, customers are demanding better service and speed. The Irish bank AIB set a goal of under ten minutes to open a new account. The investment in technology and culture change paid off with a 25% increase in accounts opened and a 20% drop in costs.

 In the digital economy, speed is the new currency; and culture is either an enabler or a barrier.

Perhaps the most far-reaching culture driver for digital transformation is customer-focus. And in the digital economy customers are demanding speed, customization, easy access and outstanding service. They have come to expect the Amazon or Zappos.com customer experience level from every company shopping experience. The good news is that companies who embrace digital technology and simultaneously reshape their internal culture drivers of customer-focus and cross-functional collaboration will not only improve the customer experience, but also drive down costs and improve overall speed of delivery. And internal customers will benefit just as much as the external customer.

Culture and Technology Working Together

The Progressive Insurance Company has recently introduced a digital telemetric speed monitoring device, Snapshot.[116] Once installed, Snapshot helps customers and the company monitor driving behavior, with the potential of reducing insurance rates for good drivers based on real-time data and not on historical or statistical accident or no-claim rates. Plus, for the insurance company the flow of real-time data helps its underwriters develop more accurate insurance rate algorithms. To launch such a product took an immense level of cross-functional cooperation inside the company and helped break down traditional functional silos.

Executives ranked silo-thinking and cross-functional barriers as the number one obstacles to a healthy digital culture.
~McKinsey & Co.

Technology, accurate data and analytical models can also be used to better align the corporate culture system with the business strategy and performance requirements. Every corporate culture system began as a collection of policies, practices, structures and work guidelines established early in the formation of a company, often based on the founder's understanding about how best to build and run a successful business. And over time, these practices and guidelines become accepted by employees as *"how we do things around here"* and in most cases, remain unchallenged.

But the fact is, most people's understanding of how to organize a business and manage people is based more on assumptions, previous experiences and *"rules of thumb"* than on actual data and facts. In the early life of the company when these assumptions and beliefs fit the context of the business and industry, the formula works. But when the business environment changes dramatically, as it has with the rise of the Internet and social media, advances in technology and modern living combined with shifting workforce values, the organization can easily find itself hampered in its ability to compete effectively by a system based on beliefs and assumptions that are no longer valid. The result can be *"cultural myopia"*, where decisions are made on closely held beliefs instead of hard data and facts.

 I believe in God; all others should bring data.
~W. Edwards Deming

For example, a commonly held belief in many companies is that poor employee performance and productivity are the result of lack of training, poor job descriptions and poor employee attitudes. Or that call center effectiveness is best evaluated using the metric of average call time, and the shorter the better. Another common business belief is that previous retail experience is the best criteria for evaluating resumes when hiring for front-line, customer-facing retail positions. In each of these examples, the application of technology, data analysis and algorithms has proven many of these established business beliefs to be false. An established corporate culture is often full of biases.

When a fast-service restaurant chain wanted to reduce turnover, which was damaging customer satisfaction levels and increasing overall costs, it used data analytics to improve employee retention.[114] And the place to start was their traditional assumptions about hiring and about what makes a good employee. Their established beliefs were that prior retail experience and an outgoing friendly personality were essential for delivering good customer service. To gather more data points and additional variables to verify their ingrained cultural beliefs, the company conducted personality profile tests on current employees, as well as gathering data on such variables as commute distance, shift length and even the performance ratings of store managers. They even attached digital sensors to employees to track movement around the restaurant, amount of time spent talking with colleagues and customers, and even the tone of their conversations.

The actual data proved insightful and shattered several of the company's long-held cultural beliefs. For example, prior retail experience had very little correlation with the quality of customer service levels or employee turnover. In fact, commute distance came out as one of the strongest drivers. And the belief that friendly, outgoing personality traits made for good customer service and employee success was replaced with data showing that a personality style of focusing on tasks and getting things done without distractions rated highest.

Even shift length had an impact on customer service, with longer shifts resulting in poorer employee service. And the quality of store management was shown to have a significant impact on customer service levels and staff turnover, not just years of experience as a store manager as had been previously believed. Using this data not only changed the way the company hired and trained employees and managers, but resulted in improved levels of customer service, reduced costs and shifted the overall store culture as well.

 At least 40% of all businesses will die in the next 10 years...
if they don't figure out how to change their entire company to
accommodate new technologies.
~John Chambers, Executive Chairman, Cisco System

Corporate Culture and the Board

 An effective board must have the wisdom to advise, the courage to look deeper, and the insight to look beyond.

The Board of Directors in a public corporation is elected by shareholders and is the highest authority in the management of the company. The Board appoints the chief executive officer and sets out the overall strategic direction. In a non-stock corporation with no general voting membership, the board is the supreme governing body.

The big conundrum for Board members today is that they need to be mature, seasoned business people with broad executive experience in order to offer sage strategic and leadership advice, while at the same time understand the modern world challenges of new technologies, cyber-crime, employee disengagement, reputational risk, shifting global economics, national and international politics, cross-cultural business issues, changing government regulation and legislation, just to name a few.

So how can the Board and individual Non-Executive Directors be more effective? An understanding of corporate culture and its impact on employee behavior and business performance may offer some key insights.

Diversity among top management and at board level, especially gender diversity, has a strong impact on company performance, yet boards and executive level positions have traditionally been highly non-diverse when it comes to gender and minority representation.[117] Women and minorities are making up a larger and larger part of purchasing decisions globally and their views as consumers, as well as their insights on business and social issues could be of great value to helping shape company strategy and business decisions.

In many ways, the beliefs, biases and habits ingrained in the corporate culture system can be a significant roadblock to management and board-level diversity. There seem to be three major points at which cultural habits and beliefs block the advancement of diversity in a company; barriers to entry, stuck in middle management, or locked out of top executive positions.[118] As a result, the quantity and quality of diverse candidates who quality for Board positions is dramatically reduced.

According to Indra Nooyi, CEO and Chairman of PepsiCo, who happens to be an Indian woman, increasing diversity at all levels, but especially at senior decision-making levels, is a *"business imperative"*, especially for a global company with a widely diverse consumer base.[119]

Culture, The Board and Strategy

Of the many responsibilities of the Board of Directors, advising on company strategy is probably the most important. A diverse Board with a wide-range of business experience is used by the CEO and executive team to develop, validate and support a company's business strategy. The expertise and input from senior board members is critical in advising management and also protecting the interests of all stakeholders from a weak or poorly developed strategy. And this role is critical to all concerned since company strategy impacts all parts of the business, especially capital expenditures and risk taking. Many Boards and Non-Executive Directors deliver great value in the establishment of company strategy.

However, a written strategy is no guarantee that it can or will be successfully delivered. Many strategies are sound, competitive, based on thorough market and customer research, yet fail to be delivered. In fact, numerous studies by McKinsey & Co. and others estimate that nearly 60% of organizations fail to deliver on their stated business strategies and objectives.

Is it faulty analytics, strong competitors, unexpected global economic events or lack of adequate capital? While these may be a factor, the most common culprit of strategy failure is poor execution. More often than not, corporate culture is the overriding factor in poor strategy execution. [135]

For Boards and Non-Executive Directors to be effective in carrying out their roles and responsibilities, it is imperative they understand and take into account the current strengths and weaknesses of the company culture. As we have shown earlier, a culture not aligned with the strategy can act as an anchor on effective strategy execution. Yet few Boards have any knowledge, information or insight into the company culture and rarely do they ask for such information, if it even exists in the company. Currently, culture is not in the Board's remit.

The Board and Risk Culture

 Most risk professionals – on the whole a highly analytical, data rational group – believe the banking crisis was caused not so much by technical failures as by failures in organizational culture and ethics. [120]

Risk oversight is an important responsibility of the Board and stands apart from risk management. However, recent regulation is being enacted that calls for independent, internal risk management functions and frameworks that must be approved by the Board or Board Risk Committee, adding another degree to just how involved the Board becomes in the management of the company. Risk is the responsibility of the full Board, not just the Audit or Risk Committee and to be most effective there should be frequent and open discussions with management and not just a policy or document in place. As we have shown earlier, culture can be a significant business risk and as such, there is ample cause for the Board to understand and review the company culture.

Regulation and compliance structures have proven to be less than effective in eliminating risky and unethical behavior within companies. In a 2010 presentation and discussion at the Society of Actuaries' Risk Symposium on *"Creating a Risk Management Culture"*, Norman Marks and Michael Rasmussen stated:

While some risk taking will be governed by rules and controls, much is governed directly by culture – where often rules and controls are not effective, fail, or are ignored.[121].

Does your Board understand the inherent risks that could reside within your current corporate culture? A better understanding by the Board of corporate culture and its inherent risks can be a valuable tool in risk oversight and mitigation.

The Audit Committee is another important element of the Board, and one that in most companies is composed solely of non-executive directors to maintain an independent oversight of financial reporting and disclosure. And the information presented to the Audit Committee should be the result of an open and transparent review and discussion with executive management. However, that is not always the case and here again we see the role of culture as a potential business risk.

Recently British Telecom shares fell 20% as a result of an accounting scandal in one of its business units resulting in a loss of £7bn in BT market value. The leadership and Board of BT admitted to *'inappropriate behavior'* by management in its Italian business from improper accounting practices, where after several years of internal investigation it was found that earnings had been overstated by £530mn.

In 2011, newly appointed Olympus Corporation CEO Michael Woodford uncovered a massive corporate accounting scandal that stretched back to the 1980's and eventually involved fraud investigations from the Serious Fraud Office, Federal Bureau of Investigation, Financial Services Agency, Tokyo Metropolitan Police, Securities and Exchange Surveillance Commission and Tokyo Stock Exchange. By 2012 the scandal had developed into one of the biggest financial scandals in the history of corporate Japan, wiped 75–80% off the company's market valuation, and led to the resignation of much of the board, the arrest of eleven past or present Directors, senior managers, auditors and bankers of Olympus for alleged criminal activities or cover-up. *The Economist* said that the Olympus scandal *"is not an accounting misdeed—it is a mindset"*. [122] The Olympus scandal is less about a single sad incident as it is a view about the malleability of rules in a corporate culture of secrecy and non-transparency.

Both these examples of cover-ups and inappropriate behavior had been going on for years either under the nose of the Board or with their knowledge. Again we can see corporate culture (the habitual way a company and its employees approach business problems and issues) implicated. It is not uncommon for a Board member or the Audit Committee to question certain issues in financial statements or management practices, only to be told by either the CFO or Chairman that *"it's an operational management issue and not a Board oversight matter!"*. When the Board is routinely excluded from digging into issues of concern, it is a big clue that a culture of transparency and openness does not exist and as a result, the corporate culture poses a potential risk for the company and its shareholders, who trust the Board to look after their financial interests.

Culture and CEO Succession

One of the most important and far reaching responsibilities of the Board of Directors is CEO succession, and a role that has profound impact on all stakeholders for years to come. With the average longevity of CEOs at around 7.5 years, added to the fact that it takes around 2-3 years to find a CEO replacement and at least 6 months to a year for a new CEO to develop a forward agenda for change, it is imperative the Board have an ongoing process to successfully manage this important change in business leadership.

Two key issues when picking a new CEO are *"fit for the culture"* and *"fit for the current situation"*, both of which must be taken into consideration for a successful replacement. Often a crisis, slowdown in sales or profits, or the entrance of new technologies and competition requires the Board to find someone capable to executing a successful business turnaround. And in such cases, many Boards opt for an outsider with proven skills in growth or turnarounds, passing over inside candidates for fear they may have overly strong ties with the current management culture and past business decisions which would keep them from taking the bold decisions and speedy action required. Yet outsiders come with a definite disadvantage and that is a lack of understanding of the corporate culture and how to get things done internally.

A recent example is the appointment of Stefan Larsson as the CEO of luxury upscale fashion retailer Ralph Laurens, replacing the founder. [123] With declining sales and rising costs, an outsider with a successful track record of business growth was chosen, only to resign abruptly two years later due to differences with the culture and the founder. Cultural fit is incredibly important and strong cultures are difficult to navigate and change. So, after two years, and a search that probably took another two years, the new outside CEO is gone, Ralph Lauren stock has taken a huge hit, and the turnaround stalled. Did the board initiate an open debate about culture as a factor in bringing in outside leadership, or did they look at credentials and ignore the strength of a culture where the founder is still very active?

The Board and Global Cultures

In the stated strategy of many firms is the direct intent to expand into new regions and take advantage of the growing opportunities presented by underdeveloped countries and emerging markets. Sound advice from the Board should be widely sought and nowhere is there a greater need for an understanding of corporate and national cultures than when making decisions about global expansion. One reason has to do with the large capital and operational risks these plans contain, but another equally important reason to take corporate and national cultures into consideration during the planning process is reputational risk. And even large companies with talented and experienced Boards can get it horribly wrong.

Ebay's failure in the Chinese market against incumbent TaoBao is a classic example of not understanding a culture in which Chinese customers prefer to develop trust through their own interactions with sellers, rather than acting on other users' ratings. And Ebay's Board is filled with tech executives but very few internationally experienced board members. Starbuck's failure in Australia is the result of a standardized, formulaic business entering a country with a culture of fierce individualism where customers preferred a friendly and original local coffee drinking experience.

Even giant Walmart has misread several foreign cultures. For example, in South Korea, the company ignored local preferences for buying small packages at local stores and the presence of native discount chains. Similar problems contributed to its closures in Germany, where customers could find groceries for lower prices at local stores and also have a local, friendly shopping experience.[124]

And when a corporate culture does not adequately stress the values of integrity and ethics but instead focuses more on profit and sales, it is not uncommon for executives and regional managers to become caught up in foreign corrupt practices. Companies that are large and complex, or with weak or fragmented corporate cultures are especially susceptible. And establishing practices, internal policies and compliance concerning the elimination of corruption and unethical practices is an important role of the Board of Directors.

Between the beginning of the global financial crisis in 2008 and today, upwards of $300 Billion in fines have been levied against global banks and financial institutions for unethical and fraudulent actions. A question that is being increasingly asked by shareholders and stakeholders alike is, what is the Board of Directors doing to ensure better behavior and governance within today's business organizations?

For Boards and Non-Executive Directors to be effective in carrying out their roles and responsibilities, it is imperative they understand and take into account the current strengths and weaknesses of the company culture. Does your Board have access to culture surveys? Are there trends, up or down, that may indicate potential business or operational risks? Do senior leaders behave in alignment with the company values and desired behaviors? Does the CEO stress culture and values at meetings and in company presentations? These are areas where it is easy for Board members to evaluate.

 When the Board spends equal time on strategy, risk, CEO succession and corporate culture, you can be guaranteed of good governance.

I am not suggesting that in every case the Board and Non-Executive Directors are accountable for the above cited ethical and management failings. The role of the board is advisory and oversight, not operational. However, the Board Chairman and Non-Executive Directors must have a greater influence on risk mitigation by asking the right questions, and demanding satisfactory answers. And many of the clues for better governance and risk mitigation have their genesis in an understanding of corporate culture.

It is time for the Board to focus on corporate culture and its impact on performance, for the benefit of all stakeholders.

 The strategy to achieve a company's purpose should reflect the values and culture of the company and should not be developed in isolation. Boards should oversee both.
~Sir Winfried Bischoff

The Board Culture

And what about the culture of the Board itself? Great Boards are more than just the sum of the expertise of its members. And all Boards have a culture, or habitual ways of working and thinking. Like the corporate culture system of an organization, the culture of the Board of Directors is a unique interplay of tangible and intangible culture drivers. Board composition, term lengths, policies concerning attendance and composition, as well as the structure of meetings and internal Board processes drive the collective behavior and performance of the Board as much as individual member personalities, levels of openness and trust, teamwork and behavioral expectations. When all these factors are aligned and in service of the stated purpose and mission of the Board, it can be an important body that effectively advises and supports management, and at the same time protects the interests of all stakeholders.

In many ways, Board culture is influenced by the Core Principle of Shadow of the Leader. In this case the leader being the Board Chairman. The degree to which the Chairman values the softer elements of effective governance often determines the difference between a healthy Board culture and a dysfunctional one. According to the UK Financial Reporting Council's report on Corporate Culture and the Role of Boards, a healthy Board culture has a high level of both challenge and support between and among its members. [125]

Boards with a healthy culture help the company establish the *"tone from the top"* and a strong leadership shadow by being serious about their own Board culture as well as the culture of the company.[126] A healthy Board culture can be characterized by:

o   the extent to which they acknowledge the importance of culture and company values,

o   behaving as role models of the culture and values,

o   how frequently company culture and values are cited in board papers and minutes,

o   when values and culture are taken into consideration during strategy and investment decisions,

o   whether or not the board encourages management to imbed values and positive cultural behaviors into the business,

o   using cultural fit and values when evaluating prospective Board members and also for evaluating current Board members,

o having regularly scheduled Board retreats that include ample time for teambuilding and alignment,

o reviewing culture surveys and making recommendations to management,

o spending time inside the company listening to employees and customers.

One has to wonder about the culture of the Board at such companies as Wells Fargo, Barings, BP, Blackberry, Kodak, Chrysler, Times Warner and others that were devastated by poor business decisions, excessive leadership behavior, or a toxic corporate culture that was either purposefully fraudulent or significantly out of touch with the market, employees and customers.

 In life and business, there are two cardinal sins, the first is to act precipitously without thought, and the second is to not act at all. Unfortunately, the board of directors and top management of Times Warner already committed the first sin by merging with AOL, and we believe they are currently in the process of committing the second; now is not a time to move slowly and suffer the paralysis of inaction. ~Carl Icahn

Building a "Global" Corporate Culture

❚❚ *As companies expand globally,*
corporate culture often lags behind

The holy grail of growth for organizations in many industries often lies outside a company's traditional footprint into emerging markets and regions. Overall, emerging markets are expected to continue to have a 3-4X higher growth rate over developed markets. While many corporations are enamored by the lure of emerging markets, which have fewer established competitors and greater opportunities for consumer spending, few companies succeed at building an organizational culture that is globally integrated and flexible enough to accommodate local variations.[127]

One exception is Yum! Brands, owner of iconic KFC, Taco Bell and Pizza Hut fast-food restaurants. Yum! Brands, headquartered in Louisville, Kentucky, does business in 117 countries with 1.4 million employees and more than 70% of its profits originating outside the United States. Over 12% of its 37,000 restaurants are located in China alone. Yum! posted an annual EPS growth rate of at least 13% between 2002 and 2012 during its accelerated global expansion.

❚❚ *When we first started our company, the single highest priority*
I had was to create a global culture where we can galvanize

---

around the behaviors that we know will drive results in our industry. ~David Knovak [128]

The leaders of Yum! Brands realized that the behaviors for success at store level were the same across all its brands and were based on the fact that employees want to work in a culture where they can add value to the customer on a daily basis and not be micromanaged or hemmed in by rigid processes and company policies. Yum! calls it *"Customer Mania"* and the culture revolves around employee recognition and peer celebrations. Store managers make recognition fun and engaging with awards like the famous rubber chicken, cheese heads and giant taco sauce packets. They even have a management award of an oversized set of walking teeth for those who *"Walk the Talk"*. And these basic human elements of recognition, peer learning, team support and adding value to the customer experience translate well across multiple cultures. And at Yum! the CEO, David Knovak designed and taught internal management workshops titled *"Taking People with You"*.

The Yum! brands phenomenal growth in China, where they opened 656 new restaurants in 2011 alone is a good example of building a global corporate culture. The key to building a global corporate culture is to identify a few basic core human behaviors that help employees grow, develop skills and receive peer and customer recognition, and then for each global region, understand the regional customer base and customer preferences. Yum! has taken Western brands like KFC and Pizza Hut with products like Original Recipe chicken and Pan Pizza and made them relevant for the Chinese consumer by extending menus with innovative products to fit local taste preferences.

 Cross-cultural competence is at the crux of a sustainable competitive advantage in a global marketplace.

Another good example of a company taking steps to integrate both corporate and local culture is McDonald's. They insist that certain standards, such as quality, cleanliness, speed and branding remain uniform across the globe. These culture drivers are not negotiable. However, McDonald's readily adapts their menus to local cultures:

o   Indonesia — rice is substituted for French fries;
o   Korea — roast pork is substituted for beef; and,
o   Germany — beer is served.

And in Hawaii, in addition to the traditional Egg McMuffin, there is a McDonalds Spam breakfast consisting of scrambled eggs, a scoop of rice and grilled Spam, a favorite Hawaiian delicacy!

Cross-Cultural Competence

Success in building cross-cultural competence lies in first understanding the specifics of national culture behavior while at the same time adapting the various drivers of corporate culture to local requirements. And here is where most companies get it wrong, thinking that the drivers of culture that work for the business in North America or Europe will be the same for other global regions. And when a culture is built on command and control and top-down management oversight to drive results locally, it is even more difficult to change when trying to run operations in regions far away from headquarters.

The *Business Model of Intercultural Analysis* is a useful framework for understanding and adapting to the business and human requirements of different national cultures. The framework uses six lenses to examine cross cultural business challenges: cultural themes, communication, group dynamics, *'glocalization',* process engineering, and time orientation. (129)

For example, in the Chinese business culture, the Confucian value of endurance and building trust over time often means that negotiations are expected to take a considerable amount of time. Western cultures on the other hand value speed and directness. This cultural disconnect can cause a loss of business opportunity when the Westerner opts out or alternatively makes price concessions too early because they are unprepared for the length of what the Chinese consider a normal negotiation.

And it is easy to make costly financial mistakes due to a misunderstanding of local cultural values and business expectations. Disney made a number of cultural mistakes when it opened Euro Disney outside of Paris that resulted in considerable financial loss and slow acceptance by local customers:

o   Naming it Euro Disney, which was a direct association with the currency and not the European culture,

o   Using plastic cutlery in a country that prides itself on its sophisticated culinary culture, o   Touting Mickey Mouse and other characters as childhood heroes at the expense of the society's actual childhood cartoon icons,

o   Ignoring the necessity of providing kennels in a culture where many families travel with dogs,

o   Having most signage in English,

o   Not offering wine with meals.

That failure to *"glocalize"*, along with other strategic culture mistakes, resulted in lower than budgeted attendance and after only two years the company was forced to borrow $175 million to keep operating.

When contemplating expanding globally, it is best to bring local executives into the planning process early, long before product, marketing and operations commitments are made. Their intimate knowledge of the subtle drivers of the national culture can save invaluable time and money. With an understanding of the core principle that culture works on human logic, not business logic, it would be wise to copy the techniques of the Toyota marketing and product design functions, who actually move in with customers for weeks on end to understand in detail how they live, how they buy, what their values are when it comes to product purchases and family life. Global customers are clamoring for more choice in products and services, but they want them presented in a culturally compatible way.

 Cross-cultural differences have time and time again been identified as the most significant impediment to successful international ventures and business projects.

Building a Future-Proof Culture

❚❚ *The most successful animals are those that can adapt to change. ~Charles Darwin*

The Arctic Hare (*Lepus arcticus*) is a very remarkable creature. Not only does it thrive and survive in the Arctic, where no other rabbit species can, but it is supremely adapted to radically different environments. In the summer it looks like a normal, gregarious rabbit, with mottled brown fur that blends in with the rocks and grasses. However, during the arctic winters its fur turns completely white, allowing it to blend in with the surrounding snow. A perfect camouflage. To me what is even more remarkable is that the fur begins to turn white before the first snows. Somehow this animal is programmed to anticipate the coming change in the environment and gets ready early!

The Arctic Hare illustrates an important concept of a future-proof, sustainable company. Business agility is the ability of management and employees to anticipate and adapt quickly in response to changing external requirements.

❚❚ *At GE, we have stayed competitive for more than 130 years because of our relentless quest for progress on all fronts, including culture. We believe that there is no such thing as a 130-year culture. ~Raghu Krishnamoorthy, Chief Learning Officer, General Electric*

Cultural Agility

Much has been written about the concept of Agility in business. There are a multitude of articles on agile software development, learning agility, leadership agility, organizational agility and process agility. In the context of corporate culture, agility relates to collective beliefs and practices that cause individuals and teams to be curious and adaptive when it comes to change, whether external or internally driven.

Korn-Ferry has conducted research showing that executives with high scores along five agility dimensions are promoted faster and deliver better performance results than those with lower agility scores. And there are even a few studies correlating high agility scores among the senior team with better business performance.[130]

Can we extend this thinking to *"cultural agility?"* Is it possible to build a system of culture drivers that can shift to adapt to a changing business environment? The answer is yes, if the drivers of culture are designed around the customer and not around traditional business drivers such as costs and profit. And critical for an agile culture is a constant flow of communications between customers, leadership and employees.

 The 'voice of the customer' should also be the 'voice of the company culture'!

When the culture drivers are customer-centric, a company not only has the ability to respond to external shifts in the marketplace, but can even anticipate those shifts well before they arrive. Like the Arctic Hare being able to sense the coming of winter and change the color of its fur before the snow arrives, the voice of the customer acts as an early warning system for marketplace shifts. A culture of agility is not easy to develop or sustain, but can be worth the effort, especially in our rapidly changing business world. It's far better than constantly playing catch-up!

A culture built around the customer places a high premium on internal communications. A 2009 report by Towers Watson of 328 organizations and five million employees worldwide found that companies with the most comprehensive internal communication efforts showed a 47 percent higher total return to shareholders.[131] *"In times of change"*, note the study's authors, *"successful companies focus on the customer and use communication programs to drive productivity, quality and safety"*.

Adaptive cultures are also notable for the behaviors they choose to minimize. There's less emphasis on being careful, predictable, avoiding conflict, and rigid budgets. Organizations that focus too heavily on standardization, optimization and driving out variability tend to underinvest in experimentation and new business models that often bring new insights in changing markets.[132]

Building and sustaining an adaptive corporate culture system not only relies on the courage of leaders to reshape business models and change culture drivers to match shifting market demands, but also relies heavily on having the right people in key positions. And that often means people with open, curious minds and a passion for continuous improvement combined with a deep concern for the customer and end user.

Cultures that collect and use real-time data on all aspects of the customer experience, combined with people obsessed with delivering value to customers tend to be the most adaptable, and the most successful.

 For many industries, the customer is now in the driver's seat.

Customer Driven Cultural Agility

Ian Davis, former Managing Partner of McKinsey & Company believes agility and adaptability are critical to long-term business success.[133]

> *"In my observation, organizations that successfully adapt over multiple product and innovation cycles demonstrate a number of characteristics:*
>
> o *relentlessly focus on their customers, and not just on their performance with customers but also on understanding what their best and most innovative customers are doing,*
>
> o *engage their key suppliers to solve problems and identify opportunities, so that these activities also become key sources of insight,*
>
> o *avoid introversion and actively seek to understand broader trends outside their own organizations and industries,*
>
> o *challenge legacy thinking and legacy mind-sets, encouraging—and tolerating the cost of—internal competition and cannibalization,*
>
> o *avoid hubris, by creating a culture of dissatisfaction with current performance, however good. Andy Grove was right—paranoia is helpful,*

o   *adopt a predominantly 'grow your own' talent philosophy to create a robust and loyal culture but mix it selectively and judiciously with external hires. In times of fundamental and disruptive change, enduring companies must be willing to change their management,*

o   *do not tolerate extended tenures in top-management roles,*

o   *focus relentlessly on values and constantly demonstrate why they matter—the values of a company, to be meaningful, must be reflected in the key managerial processes, such as performance evaluation and appointments. A company's values are judged by actions and behavior, not words and mission statements,*

o   *meaningfully and purposefully engage younger generations in formulating policy and organizational development, both to stimulate innovation and to prevent generational barriers. Conversely, new tech companies in Silicon Valley might think more about how to engage older managerial generations,*

o   *encourage their boards to play an active—but supportive—role in challenging priorities and the status quo, particularly in times of success.*

Agility not only allows a company to reach the future faster than others, but it also allows them to shape markets as well.[134] Consider the new emerging markets made possible by Apple and Microsoft in the 70s and 80s as compared to IBM and Xerox during that time. Agile and adaptive companies not only develop products for the future, they also develop talent capable of capitalizing on that invented future.

 Future proofing your organization means being more interested in what's possible than what's profitable.
~Sara Roberts

Agile, future poof cultures share many similarities not found in traditional companies. They believe it is better to be fast than big. Speed is their currency, not size. Profits are reinvested in risky new opportunities rather than handed out in bonuses or hoarded. They focus more on the external environment than on internal issues and opportunity trumps politics. They welcome outsiders who bring new ideas and ways of working. They are always hungry for new challenges and constantly thinking of ways to make a great product or service even greater. Their hiring profiles are based on future needs, not past success. They believe more in their business purpose than their business strategy. Purpose allows them to adapt and shift direction and business models. And in most cases of agile, future-proof cultures, that purpose is the customer.

 No man ever steps in the same river twice, for it's not the same river and he's not the same man. ~Heraclitus

Epilogue

Seven Corporate Culture Questions Every Business Executive Should Ask

I like questions. Questions make people think. Statements may go in one ear and out the other, but a good question will bounce around inside your head until you come up with an answer. And good questions often breed even better questions. The outcome of all those questions is often a new insight.

Executives have been trained to make statements, to deliver facts and information via PowerPoint and to overwhelm others with massive spreadsheets few can understand. It's what I call *"razzle - dazzle"* management. Energetic and impressive, but not really educational or insightful. And PowerPoints don't drive performance!

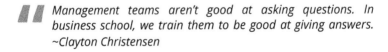 *Management teams aren't good at asking questions. In business school, we train them to be good at giving answers.*
~Clayton Christensen

Education comes from the Latin word, *"educo"* which roughly translated means to draw out. Real education then comes from the ability to draw out insights and answers from the student rather than pour in facts and data. And one of the best ways to draw out new insights for the learner is to ask questions! Some call it the Socratic method. I call it the leadership method.

Here are some of the most important questions you should be asking about corporate culture:

1. What is the business case for culture in our company?

Before you can really use the power of culture as a business value driver, it is important to understand the *"cost of a poor culture"* and the business benefits of a corporate culture system aligned with your business strategies. One of the ways to get your team to understand the business case for culture is to talk about how cultural barriers such as poor cross functional handoffs, lack of transparency, not following up with teammates in a timely manner, resistance to new ways of working, lack of innovation, and other cultural behaviors get in the way of project delivery and execution on important strategic initiatives. In the case of the recent incident at United Airlines where a passenger was forcibly removed due to overbooking, the market value of the stock was reduced by $1.8 billion. That's a big case for culture.

Another broad rule of thumb is to ask your team what percentage, on average, of a productive day's work is lost through blaming, finger-pointing, slow responses, lack of trust of other departments, poor teamwork, poor customer service, etc. Usually the number is around 30%. Take your total employee cost figure, including benefits, and multiply it by that number (say 30%) and you will get an estimate of the cost of a poor culture. It's a staggering figure in most cases. And even a slight improvement falls straight to the bottom line!

2. Is our culture an asset or a liability? How would we know?

Does your team know the current strengths and weaknesses of your current culture? Have they done a culture assessment? Have they held conversations with their team about the strengths and weaknesses of the culture? Can you identify the culture barriers to improved strategy execution? In what way is our current culture a competitive advantage? A competitor can copy your products and services, but they can't copy your unique culture. But if they could, would they really want to?

3. Is building and sustaining a high-performance culture a part of our formal, written business strategy?

When an initiative shows up on the formal strategy document, signed off by the Board, and specific accountabilities get assigned, more often than not those initiatives get funded and resourced. Have you made a High-Performance Culture one of your key business strategic initiatives? Do you have specific plans with milestones and deliverables against this initiative? Is it properly funded or just a "hope to improve" item? What gets measured and reported often gets done!

4. Is alignment with culture and values a part of our hiring, performance reviews, bonuses and promotions?

In many companies, values and behaviors are just words on the wall or in the employee handbook and have little impact on the day-to-day work. By putting culture and values as a significant part of performance reviews, promotional criteria and bonuses, they suddenly become more important. And if the scores are given through a 360-degree evaluation process, they have even more power to influence behavior.

5. Have we mapped the various subcultures and their alignment with the overall strategy and culture of our business?

One of the most important insights into corporate culture is that most companies are composed of numerous subcultures rather than one overall corporate culture. And these subcultures can be strong influencers of *"how things get done around here"*. If you don't understand the subcultures inside your company, then you really don't understand your operational culture. In some cases, subcultures are strongly aligned with the vision, values and business strategies. And in other cases they present significant barriers to productivity and positive change.

6. Do we as a senior team talk about culture as often as we talk about costs, profit and business performance?

Much of corporate culture is developed through stories and the things people talk about the most. Stories of highly creative or accountable individuals are often told to new employees long after the individuals have retired or left. Stories contain the viral seeds for sustaining your culture. If the senior team routinely talks about sales, costs and profits, but not about values and cultural behaviors, the few times culture is mentioned it will be discounted, because everyone *"knows how important costs are to management, not culture"*.

7. Does our new employee hiring and on-boarding process help people understand our required culture and why it is important?

When was the last time the senior team sat through a new employee indoctrination process? Too often these are becoming menu driven digital exercises and few companies put much emphasis on expected behaviors and culture. It is important to remember that if you don't indoctrinate new employees, at all levels, in the company culture, they will bring their old company culture with them as their default way of working. And when many employees come on board without a good acculturation process, you will wind up with a very fragmented culture.

And a bonus question:

These 7 questions, as provocative as they are, often lead to even better questions being asked and explored by your leadership team and will undoubtedly spark a new focus in everyone on the importance of culture to your business success.

Bonus: How often do we have open debates and reviews of our culture and values?

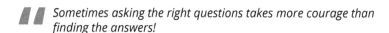 *Sometimes asking the right questions takes more courage than finding the answers!*

Summary

 Computers are magnificent tools for the realization of our dreams, but no machine can replace the human spark of spirit, compassion, love, and understanding.
~Louis V. Gerstner, Jr.

If you have made it this far in this book, then hopefully you will be taking back to your organization some new insights and ideas about the cultural levers for business success, customer delight and employee engagement. Nothing is easy, especially growing a business and leading others. It is my hope that insight into the 10 Core Principles of Corporate Culture, along with the discussions in this book of how they can be applied to the many challenges of growing a successful business, will be useful for you and your company. I also hope that some of the success stories and examples have added some inspiration and encouragement.

 The journey is the reward. ~Steve Jobs

I encourage you to pick one or two principles or examples from this book to start using in your organization or with your team right away. Apply the principles to your own life. Adapt them to fit your personal or company challenges. Remember, not all drivers in the corporate culture system have the same weight and impact. And even though the principles apply to every organization, not all organization cultures are the same. Make sure yours is aligned with the customer and your business strategy.

Before you go, here is short review of the key ideas contained in *Culture Rules!*

o   Culture and strategy are two sides of the same coin and aligned and working together they have great impact on business performance.

o   Corporate culture is a significant driver of economic business value.

o   Running an organization without an understanding of corporate culture is like driving a speeding car using only the rear view mirror.

o   Corporate Culture is like the water in a fish tank. Let it go foul and everything suffers

o   Competitors can hire your people and copy your strategy, but they can't copy your culture.

o   Adding culture interventions to traditional performance improvement programs delivers greater results.

o   Habitual culture behaviors and ways of working are not the culture, but the outcome of the corporate culture system, made up of multiple drivers. These are the levers for change.

o   Peer pressure is the strongest culture driver. Written value statements are often the weakest.

o   The 10 Core Principles of Corporate Culture

      o   Principle One: Every Organization Has a Culture

      o   Principle Two: Culture Impacts Performance

      o   Principle Three: Culture Can Be a Significant Business Risk

      o   Principle Four: Culture Works on Human Logic, Not Business Logic

      o   Principle Five: Organizations are Shadows of Their Leaders

      o   Principle Six: Cultural Drift

      o   Principle Seven: Policies Drive Culture More Than We Realize.

      o   Principle Eight: You Get the Culture You Ignore

- o Principle Nine: There Is No Perfect Corporate Culture

- o Principle Ten: Leaders and Employees Change Cultures, Not Consultants

o Culture can be an early warning system. An organization that waits for a significant downturn in financial measures such as growth and profit to signal the need for change is doomed to fail.

o If you don't manage your culture, it will manage you. Culture is a strong, invisible force that determines how people work and think.

o Culture is the only competitive advantage that is completely within your control.

o All initiatives must pass through the Jaws of Culture. And most don't make it!

o Many organizations get into trouble not because of a failed strategy, but because of a rigid culture.

o Risk comes from not knowing what your culture is doing.

o Corporate culture shouldn't happen by accident, and if it does, there could be an accident.

o Organizations may be hierarchies in paper, but they are actually social networks with subcultures led by key informal leaders.

o The most powerful leadership tool you have is your own personal example.

o The larger an organization becomes, the less influence the leaders have. Peer pressure and subcultures determine the culture more than senior leaders.

o Organizations are shadows of their leaders ... that's the good news and the bad news!

o Cultures fragment is they are not managed carefully.

o Change policies and your change behaviors.

o Leaders get the culture they deserve

o Cultures are sustained when you ignore coachable moments.

o Your culture is your brand. Customers may see your brand advertisements, but they experience your culture.

o Don't try to change corporate culture, instead change the drivers of culture.

o All successful culture change approaches have two things in common: courageous leadership and employees taking accountability for the culture.

o It takes a village to raise a child. It takes all employees to reshape culture.

o All corporate cultures a built from the same core principles, but not all cultures are the same.

o Understanding the leadership culture is the new CEO's secret weapon.

o Not all cultures scale. Growth can often dilute or destroy a good culture.

o Corporate culture is not an initiative; it is the internal business system that either supports or derails all initiatives.

o Whether by design or default, you will have a corporate culture.

o Culture clash is a key barrier to M&A and successful business integration.

o Culture change is the foundation for a sustainable business turnaround.

o In every company there is buried treasure: human treasure.

o It's not hard to make good business decisions when you understand your culture and know what your values are.

o If you want your values to be real, imbed them in every aspect of the corporate culture system.

o A corporate culture system designed around the customer has a high probability of delivering and sustaining business success.

o While organizations may be shadows of their leaders, culture at the employee level is often a shadow of middle management!

o Trust as a key driver of a culture of strong employee engagement and superior business performance.

o A culture of innovation and customer focus is a powerful lever for sustainability and competitive advantage.

o Organizational culture is one of the main barriers to company success in the digital age.

- o   Entering the digital economy cannot wait until the culture is right.

- o   Executives ranked silo-thinking and cross-functional barriers as the number one obstacles to a healthy digital culture.

- o   The Board Culture has a significant impact on the performance of a company.

- o   When the Board spends equal time on strategy, risk, CEO succession and corporate culture, you can be guaranteed of good governance.

- o   Cross-cultural competence is at the crux of a sustainable competitive advantage in a global marketplace.

- o   The *"voice of the customer"* should also be the *"voice of the company culture!"*

I believe strongly that business can and should be a force for good. A positive force for making the world a better place to work, live and fulfill our potential in a healthy and sustainable manner. Corporate culture is one of the strongest levers to make that a reality.

About John R Childress

John R. Childress is a pioneer in the field of corporate culture, strategy execution, executive leadership and organization effectiveness, author of several books and numerous articles on leadership, and an effective public speaker and workshop facilitator for boards and senior executive teams.

Between 1974 and 1978 John was Vice President for Education and a senior workshop leader with PSI World, Inc. a public educational organization. In 1978 John co-founded the Senn-Delaney Leadership Consulting Group, the first international consulting firm to focus exclusively on culture change, leadership development and senior team alignment, and served as President and CEO from 1978-2001.

His work with senior leadership teams has included companies in crisis (GPU Nuclear – owner of the Three Mile Island Nuclear Plants following the accident), deregulated industries (natural gas pipelines, telecommunications and the breakup of The Bell Telephone Companies), mergers and acquisitions, and classic business turnaround assignments with global organizations from the Fortune 500 and FTSE 250 ranks. He has designed and conducted leadership workshops and led culture change assignments for senior leadership teams in the US, UK, Europe, Middle East, Africa, China, Australia and Asia.

After retiring to France in 2001 John turned his hand to writing thriller novels. In 2004, he began to work again on consulting and coaching assignments with senior executive teams on culture change, leadership team alignment and strategy execution. His two business books, *LEVERAGE: The CEO's Guide to Corporate Culture*, and *FASTBREAK: The CEO's Guide to Strategy Execution* are considered must reads for business leaders.

John was born in the Cascade Mountains of Oregon and eventually moved to Carmel Highlands, California during most of his early business career. John is a Phi Beta Kappa scholar with a BA degree (Magna cum Laude) from the University of California, a Master's Degree from Harvard University and was a PhD candidate at the University of Hawaii before deciding on a career as a business entrepreneur in the mid-70s. In 1968-69, he attended the American University of Beirut and it was there that his interest in cultures, leadership and group dynamics began to take shape.

John currently resides in London with his family and is an avid fly fisherman, with recent trips to the Amazon River, Tierra del Fuego, and Kamchatka in the far east of Russia. He is a trustee for Young Virtuosi, a foundation to support talented young musicians.

You can reach John at: john@johnrchildress.com

For speaking engagements and keynote addresses, please contact Jerry Miller at jerry@speakerconsultantservices.com.

References

1   McCracken, Jeffrey (2006, Jan. 23). "'Way Forward' Requires Culture Shift at Ford". *The Wall Street Journal*.

2   Deloitte (2016). *Global Human Capital Trends Report*. Deloitte University Press. https://dupress.deloitte.com

3   Corkery, Michael (2016, Sep. 8) "Wells Fargo Fined $185 Million for Fraudulently Opening Accounts". *New York Times Online: Deal Book*.

4   Deloitte Australia (2014). *Get out of your own way: Unleashing productivity*. Deloitte Touche Tohmatsu. https://www2.deloitte.com/au/

5   Hyken, Shep (2017, May 6). "United Airlines: One Month Later". *Forbes.com*

6   Terkel, Amanda (2011, Aug. 8). "Delta Charges U.S. Troops Returning From Afghanistan $2,800 In Baggage Fees". *Huffington Post*

7   Childress, John R. (2013). *Leverage: The CEO's Guide to Corporate Culture*. London: The Principia Press.

8   The Economist (2014, Jan. 11). "Learning the Lingo". *The Economist* 410:8889.

9   Jaques, Elliott (1951). *The Changing Culture of a Factory: A Study of Authority and Participation in an Industrial Setting*. London: Tavistock.

10   Kotter, John P. and James L. Heskett (1992). *Corporate Culture and Performance*. New York: The Free Press.

11   Schein, Edgar M (2004). *Organizational Culture and Leadership*. Third Edition. San Francisco: Jossey-Bass.

12   Hofstede, Gert and Gert Jan Hofstede (2004). *Cultures and Organizations: Software for the Mind*. Second Edition. New York: McGraw-Hill.

13   Human Synergistics. "How Culture Works". *Humansynergistics.com*

14   Deloitte (2016). *Global Human Capital Trends Report*. Deloitte University Press.

15   Graham, John R., Campbell R, Harvey, Jillian Popadak, and Shiva Rajgopal (2016). "Corporate Culture: Evidence from the Field". *Duke Fuqua School of Business*.

16   Keller, Scott and Carolyn Aiken (N.D.). "On Performance Culture". *McKinsey & Company*.

17   Aiken, Carolyn, Scott Keller and Michael Rennie (N.D.). "The Performance Culture Imperative". *McKinsey & Company*.

18   Rucci, Anthony J., Steven P. Kirn and Richard T. Quinn (1998, January). "The Employee-Customer-Profit Chain at Sears". *Harvard Business Review*.

19   Flamholtz, Eric (2001). "Corporate Culture and the Bottom Line". *European Management Journal* 19:3, pp. 268-275.

20   Ogbonna, Emmanuel and Lloyd C. Harris (2000). "Leadership style, organizational culture and performance: empirical evidence from UK companies". *International Journal of Human Resource Management* 11:4, pp. 766-788.

21   Carucci, Ron (2017, May 29). "How Corporate Values Get Hijacked and Misused". *Harvard Business Review*

22   Schulz, John (2013, Jun. 22). "Culture, a Definition". *TorbenRick*.

23   Smith, Geoffrey and Roger Parloff (2016, Mar. 7). "Hoaxwagen: How the massive diesel fraud incinerated VW's reputation – and will

hobble the company for years to come". *Fortune.*

24   Hamel, Gary and Michele Zanini (2017, May 16). "Assessment: Do you know how bureaucratic your organization is?" *Harvard Business Review.*

25   Ohno, Taichi and Norman Bodek (1988, Mar. 1). "Toyota Production System: Beyond Large-Scale Production". *Productivity Press.*

26   Bethune, Gordon M. and Scott Huler (1998). *From Worst to First: Behind the scenes of Continental's remarkable comeback.* USA: John Wiley & Sons.

27   Martinuzzi, Bruna (2012). "What Culture is Right for your Business?" *American Express Open Forum.*

28   Heskett, James L (2011). "Managing the Culture Cycle". *World Financial Review,* pp. 1-7.

29   Boyce, Anthony S., Levi R. G. Nieminen, Michael A. Gillespie, Ann Marie Ryan and Daniel R. Denison (2015). "Which comes first, organizatonal culture or performance?" *Journal of Organizational Behavior, Volume 36, Issue 3, pp.339-359.*

30   Sheridan, John E. (1992). "Organizational culture and employee retention". *Academy of Management Journal* 35:5, pp. 1036-1056.

31   Boushey, Heather and Sarah Jane Glynn (2012). "There are Significant Business Costs to Replacing Employees". *Center for American Progress.*

32   Kantor, Judy and David Streitfield (2015, Aug. 15). "Inside Amazon: Wrestling Big Ideas in a Bruising Workplace". *New York Times,* A1.

33   Webb, Tim (2010, May 13). "BP Boss Admits Job on the Line over Gulf oil spill". *The Guardian.*

34   Mouawad, Jad and Clifford Krauss (2010, June 3). "Another Torrent BP Works to Stem: Its C.E.O". *The New York Times.*

35   U.S. Government (2011). Deep *Water: the Gulf Oil Disaster and the Future of Offshore Drilling.* The Report of the National Commission on the BP Deepwater Horizon Oil Spill and Offshore Drilling.

36   Strategy& (2016). 2016 CEO Success Study. *PWC.*

37   Leveson, Nancy (2011). "Risk Management in the Oil and Gas Industry". Testimony before the United States Senate Committee on Energy and Natural Resources, May 17, 2011. http://energy.mit.

edu/

38 Novak, Dan, Mark Rennaker and Paulette Turner (2011). "Using Organizational Network Analysis to Improve Integration Across Organizational Boundaries". *HR People & Strategy, Volume 34/Issue 4, pp. 32-37*

39 Maskin, Eric (2016, Oct.). "Leadership and behavior: Mastering the mechanics of reason and emotion". *McKinsey Quarterly*.

40 D'Alessandro, Carianne (2017). "Dropbox's CEO Was Late to a Companywide Meeting on Punctuality. What Followed Wasn't Pretty". *Inc.*

41 Zook, Chris and James Allen (2016). "Barriers and Pathways to Sustainable Growth: Harnessing the Power of the Founder's Mentality". *Bain & Co.*

42 Williams, Richard, Wallace Higgins and Harvey Greenberg (2011). "The Impact of Leader Behavior on Employee Health: Lessons for Leadership Development". *Northeast Human Resources Association*.

43 DuBois, Shelly (2013, Aug. 29). "Merrill Lynch Settles Discrimination Lawsuit". *USA Today*.

44 Ellis, Charles D (2013). *What it Takes: Seven secrets of success from the world's greatest professional firms.* Hoboken, NJ: Wiley.

45 Maanen, J. V. and S. R. Barley (1985). "Cultural Organization: Fragments of a Theory", in P. J. Frost, L. F. Moore, M. R. Louis, C. C. Lundberg and J. Martin. *Organizational Culture*. Beverly Hills: Sage, pp. 31-53.

46 John Meyer and Laryssa Topolnytsky (2000). "Organizational Culture and Retention". In *Best Practices: Employee Retention*. Toronto: Carswell.

47 Kuhn, Kristine M. (2009). "Compensation as a signal of organizational culture: the effects of advertising individual or collective incentives". *International Journal of Human Resource Management* 20:7, pp. 1634-1648.

48 Matson, Eric (1996). "The Seven Sins of Deadly Meetings". *Fast Company*.

49 Pappas, Christopher (2017, May). "Leadership Q&A: A CEO's Role in Corporate Culture". *CEP Magazine*.

50 Cave, Daniel (2017, Aug. 14). "Apple's 11 Rules for Success for New

Employees". *Business Grapevine blog.*

51   Deloitte Consulting Research (2003). *Core Beliefs and Culture Survey.* Culture of Purpose: A Business Imperative. *Deloitte.*

52   Katzenbach, Jon and DeAnne Aguirre (2013). "Culture and the Chief Executive". *strategy+business* 71.

53   Katzenbach, Jon and Paul Leinwand (2015). 'Culture eats strategy for breakfast' webinar. *Strategy&.* https://www.strategyand.pwc.com/

54   Hall, Emma (2014, Dec. 16). "Volvo will try to reinvent auto marketing with a new strategy". *AdvertisingAge.*

55   Taylor, Bill (2010, Sep. 27). "Brand is Culture, Culture is Brand". *Harvard Business Review.*

56   Smith, Martin E. (2002). "Success rates for different types of organizational change". *Performance Improvement* 41:1, pp. 26-33.

57   Aiken, Carolyn and Scott Keller (2009, April). "The Irrational Side of Change Management". *McKinsey Quarterly.*

58   Wagner, Mark and Wayne Orvis (2013, Autumn). "Changing Structures and Behaviors at Walgreens". *strategy+business* 72.

59   Herrero, Leandro (2011). *Homo Imitans.* London: Meeting Minds.

60   Masters, Brooke (2009, Mar. 30). "Rise of a headhunter". *Financial Times*

61   Nawaz, Sabina (2017, May 15). "The Biggest Mistake New Executives Make". *Harvard Business Review.*

62   Birshan, Michael, Thomas Meakin and Kurt Strovink (2016, May). "How new CEOs can boost their odds of success". *McKinsey Quarterly.*

63   Campbell, Andrew and Jo Whitehead (2009, Spring). "Think again – how good leaders can avoid bad decisions". *360°: The Ashridge Journal*, pp. 6-11.

64   Christensen, Clayton (1997). *The Innovator's Dilemma: When New Technologies Cause Great Firms to Fail.* Harvard Business School Press.

65   Nucor. "Culture". *Nucor Corporation Website*

66   Kauflin, Jeff (2017, May 9). "America's Best Employers 2017". *Forbes.*

67   Korn Ferry (2014, Sept. 8). "Korn Ferry Executive Survey: Companies Struggle to Align Culture with Business Strategy". Korn Ferry

68   McKinsey & Company (2008). "Improving Strategic Planning: A McKinsey Survey". *McKinsey Quarterly*.

69   Zook, Chris and James Allen (2016, July 20). "Barriers and Pathways to Sustainable Growth: Harnessing the Power of the Founder's Mentality". *Bain*.

70   Chatman, Jennifer A., David F. Caldwell, Charles A. O'Reilly and Bernadette Doerr (2014). "Parsing organizational culture: How the norm for adaptability influences the relationship between culture consensus and financial performance in high-technology firms". *Journal of Organizational Behavior* 35, pp. 785–808.

71   Dewhurst, Martin, Suzanne Heywood, and Kirk Reickhoff (2011, May). "Preparing your organization for growth". *McKinsey Quarterly*.

72   Hastings, Reed. "The Nexflix Culture". *Netflix.com*.

73   Amazon. "Principles". *Amazon.com*.

74   Holton, Glyn (2014). "Barings Debacle". Glyn Holton blog, www.glynholton.com

75   Bank of England (1995). *Board of Banking Supervision investigation into the failure of Barings*, London: Bank of England.

76   Lewis, Alan and Dan McKone (2016, May 10). "So many M&A deals fail because companies overlook this simple strategy". *Harvard Business Review*.

77   Stafford, Dale and Laura Miles (2013, December 11). "Integrating cultures after a merger". *Bain*.

78   Davis, Danny A. (2012). *M&A Integration: How to do it*. New York: John Wiley & Sons.

79   Kanter, Rosabeth Moss (2003, June). "Leadership and the Psychology of Turnarounds". *Harvard Business Review*.

80   Yakola, Doug (2014, March). "Ten tips for leading companies out of crisis". *McKinsey Quarterly*.

81   Bossidy, Larry and Ram Charan (2002). *Execution: The Discipline of Getting Things Done*. Crown Publications.

82   Kosur, James (2015, Oct. 5). "GE runs an intense 5-year program to develop executives, and only 2% finish it". *Business Insider UK*.

83   The Wharton School (2012, Mar. 28). "Why External Hires Get Paid More, and Perform Worse, than Internal Staff". *Knowledge@Wharton*.

84   Pierce, James G (2010). *Is the organizational culture of the U.S. Army congruent with the professional development of its senior level officer corps?* Carlisle, PA: Strategic Studies Institute, U.S. Army War College.

85   Dvorak, Nate and Bailey Nelson (2016). "Few Employees Believe in Their Company's Values". *Gallup Business Journal*.

86   Johnson&Johnson corporate website

87   Davis, Ian (2014, September). "Reflections on corporate longevity". *McKinsey Quarterly*.

88   Mankins, Michael (2004, Sept.). "Stop Wasting Valuable Time". *Harvard Business Review*.

89   American Express (2014). "Customers Reward Outstanding Service by Spending More and Spreading the Word to Friends and Family". *Americanexpress.com*.

90   "Why is Nordstrom known for their good customer service?" *Quora.com*.

91   Earl, Donna (2004). "What is Internal customer service? A definition and case study". *Donna Earl Training*.

92   Bulgyo, Zach (2013). "Tony Hsieh, Zappos, and the Art of Great Company Culture". *Kissmetrics.*

93   Heskett, James L, Thomas O. Jones, Gary W. Loveman, W. Earl Sasser, Jr., and Leonard A. Schlesinger (2008, Summer). "Putting the Service-Profit Chain to Work". *Harvard Business Review*.

94   Markey, Rob and Fred Reichheld (2012, Mar. 23). "The Economics of Loyalty". *Bain.*

95   Performance Improvement Council (N.D.). "The Economics of Customer Retention". *Incentive Marketing Association*.

96   Reichheld, Frederick F. and W. Earl Sasser, Jr. (1990, Autumn). "Zero Defections: Quality Comes to Services". *Harvard Business Review*.

97   Garvin, David A (2013, Dec.). "How Google sold its engineers on management". *Harvard Business Review*.

98   Schneider, Michael (2017, Jun. 20). "Google Employees Weighed

In on What Makes a Highly Effective Manager (Technical Expertise Came in Last)". *Inc.*

99   Brown, David, Vernoical Melian and Marc Solow (2015). "Culture and engagement: The naked organization". *Deloitte University Press.*

100   Crabtree, Steve (2013). "Worldwide, 13% of employees are engaged at work". *Gallup.*

101   Deloitte proprietary research conducted with Glassdoor, November 2014. Cited in Brown, David, Vernoical Melian and Marc Solow (2015),. "Culture and engagement: The naked organization", *Deloitte University Press.*

102   Aon Hewitt (2017). "How is Global Uncertainty Impacting Employee Engagement Levels?" *Aon Hewitt.*

103   Covey, Stephen M.R. (2006). *The Speed of Trust.* New York: Free Press.

104   Applebaum, Eileen, Thomas Bailey, Peter Berg and Arne L. Kalleberg (2000). *Manufacturing Advantage: Why High Performance Work Systems Pay Off.* Ithaca: Cornell University Press.

105   Edelman Intelligence (2017). "2017 Executive Summary". *Edelman. com.*

106   Dill, Kathryn (2014, Aug. 22). "The Top Companies for Culture and Values". *Forbes.*

107   Hanger Group (2015). "The J.E. Hanger Story". Hanger.com

108   Jarulzelski, Barry, John Loehr and Richard Holman (2011, Winter). "The Global Innovation 1000: Why Culture is Key". *strategy+business* 65.

109   Tellis, Gerard J., Jaideep C. Prabhu and Rajesh K. Chandy (2009, Jan.). "Radical Innovation Across Nations: The Preeminence of Corporate Culture". Journal of Marketing, Vol. 73, pp. 3-23.

110   Barsh, Joanna , Marla M. Capozzi, and Jonathan Davidson (2008, Jan.). "Leadership and Innovation". *McKinsey Quarterly.*

111   Geldenhuys, Tanya (2006). *Organisational Culture as A Predictor Of Performance: A Case Study In Liberty Life.* MBA dissertation, University of Pretoria, SA.

112   Boston Consulting Group (2014). *The Most Innovative Companies 2014: Breaking through is hard to do.* BCG Perspectives.

113 Ohr, Ralph (2016, Sept. 5). "Innovation and Organizational Culture". *Innovation Excellence.*

114 Arellano, Carla, Alexander DiLeonardo, and Ignatio Felix (2017, July). "Using people analytics to drive business performance: A case study". *McKinsey Quarterly.*

115 BMC Software (2017, Jan. 18). "World Economic Forum: Facing new digital demands, 88 percent of employees place responsibility for creating innovative cultures on employers". *Newsroom.bmc.com*

116 Harvard Business School (2016, Nov. 16). "Getting Smart: How Progressive Is Deploying Data To Win in Auto Insurance". *Harvard Business School Open Knowledge.* https://rctom.hbs.org/

117 McKinsey & Company (2007, Oct.). "Gender Diversity, a Corporate Performance Driver". *McKinsey.*

118 Krivovich, Alexis, Eric Kutcher, and Lareina Yee (2016, Mar.). "Breaking down the gender challenge". *McKinsey Quarterly.*

119 Clifford, Catherine (2016, Oct. 17). "PepsiCo CEO: Hiring more women and people of color is a 'business imperative". *CNBC.*

120 Moore, Carter, and Associates (2009). "The RiskMinds 2009 Risk Managers Survey: The causes and implications of the 2008 banking crisis". *RiskMinds.*

121 Marks, Norman and Michael Rasmussen (2010). "Creating a RiskManagement Culture". Presentation delivered at the 2010 Society of Actuaries Risk Symposium.

122 Banyan (2012, Feb. 16). "The Olympus Scandal: Arrested development". *The Economist.*

123 Haapaniemi, Peter (2017, Jul. 26). "Ralph Lauren Reaches Across Industry Boundaries for a New CEO". *Chief Executive.*

124 Landler, Mark and Michael Barbaro (2006, Aug. 2). "Wal-Mart Finds that its Formula Doesn't Fit Every Culture". *New York Times.*

125 UK Financial Reporting Council (2016, July). "Corporate Culture and the Role of Boards". *United Kingdom, Financial Reporting Council.*

126 Carey, Anthony (2017). "Board culture - Its role in achieving sustainable success". *United Kingdom, Mazars Publications.*

127 Levy, Orly, Sully Taylor and Nakiye A. Boyacigiller (2010, Summer). "On the Rocky Road to Strong Global Culture". MIT Sloan

Management Review.

128 Reiss, Robert (2012, Mar. 5). "Driving a global corporate culture of 1.4 million employees". *Forbes.*

129 Hummel, Denise Pirrotti (2012, May). "Understanding the Importance of Culture in a Global Business". *Profit Magazine.*

130 Korn Ferry (2014). "Korn Ferry Study Finds Companies with Highly Agile Executives have 25 Percent Higher Profit Margins". *Korn Ferry.*

131 Towers Watson (2009). "2009/2010 Communication ROI Study Report: Capitalizing on Effective Communication". *Willis Towers Watson.*

132 Ohr, Ralph (2016, Sept. 5). "Innovation and Organizational Culture". *Innovation Excellence.*

133 Davis, Ian (2014, Sept.). "Reflections on corporate longevity". *McKinsey Quarterly.*

134 Roberts, Sara (2016, Nov.). "Future-Proofing Through Culture: An organizational manifesto". *Speakers' Spotlight.*

135 Childress, John R (2014). *FASTBREAK: The CEO's Guide to Strategy Execution.* The Principia Press

136 Kegan, Robert, Lisa Lahey, Matthew Miller, Andy Fleming and Deborah Helsing (2016). *An Everyone Culture: Becoming a Deliberately Developmental Organization.* Boston: Harvard Business Review Press

CPSIA information can be obtained
at www.ICGtesting.com
Printed in the USA
LVHW012351211218
601122LV00006B/7